TEACHER'S PET PUBLICATIONS

LITPLAN TEACHER PACK
for
The Miracle Worker
based on the play by
William Gibson

Written by
Janine H. Sherman

© 1998 Teacher's Pet Publications
All Rights Reserved

This **LitPlan** for William Gibson's
The Miracle Worker
has been brought to you by Teacher's Pet Publications, Inc.

Copyright Teacher's Pet Publications 1998
11504 Hammock Point
Berlin MD 21811

Only the student materials in this unit plan (such as worksheets, study questions, and tests) may be reproduced multiple times for use in the purchaser's classroom.

For any additional copyright questions, contact Teacher's Pet Publications.

www.tpet.com

TABLE OF CONTENTS - *The Miracle Worker*

Introduction	5
Unit Objectives	8
Reading Assignment Sheet	9
Unit Outline	10
Study Questions (Short Answer)	13
Quiz/Study Questions (Multiple Choice)	22
Pre-reading Vocabulary Worksheets	37
Lesson One (Introductory Lesson)	53
Nonfiction Assignment Sheet	55
Oral Reading Evaluation Form	65
Writing Assignment 1	54
Writing Assignment 2	57
Writing Assignment 3	73
Writing Evaluation Form	70
Vocabulary Review Activities	80
Extra Writing Assignments/Discussion ?s	75
Optional Project	81
Unit Review Activities	82
Unit Tests	85
Unit Resource Materials	125
Vocabulary Resource Materials	149

A FEW NOTES ABOUT THE AUTHOR
William Gibson

GIBSON, William (1914-). Playwright and poet, William Gibson, was born on November 13, 1914 in New York, New York. He attended the College of City of New York (now City College of the City University of New York) from 1930-1932. The former piano teacher married his second wife, Margaret Brenaman, a psychoanalyst, on September 6, 1940. During the late 1940's he and his wife Margaret spent time in Kansas; she doing post-graduate work at Menniger; he doing research for his writing at Kansas University. While there he served on the Board and acted with the Topeka Civic Theatre. He was known to play jazz piano in East Topeka.

William Gibson also wrote under the pseudonym, William Mass. His awards and honors include: The Harriet Monroe Memorial Prize 1945, for a group of poems published in *Poetry*, The Topeka Civic Theatre award, 1947, for *A Cry of Players*, and the Sylvania Award, 1957 for the television play, "The Miracle Worker." While he has written over twenty-five plays and a variety of poetry, fiction, and criticisms; he is best known for his 1957 play, *The Miracle Worker*. Originally written and performed as a television drama, it was later adapted for the stage, screen, and again for television in 1979. It has been deemed "one of the most assuredly affirmative dramatic works to come out of the optimistic 50's."

In 1982 Gibson returned to the characters of *The Miracle Worker* with the play *Monday After the Miracle*. Helen, now 21 years old, has entered college, with Annie Sullivan accompanying her as translator and tutor. It did not receive the acclaim of its predecessor, but has been called "At the very least a well-made play." He has been president and co-founder of the Berkshire Theatre Festival in Stockbridge and makes Stockbridge, Massachusetts his home. He has two sons, Thomas and Daniel.

INTRODUCTION - *The Miracle Worker*

This unit has been designed to develop students' reading, writing, thinking, and language skills through exercises and activities related to *The Miracle Worker* by William Gibson. It includes twenty lessons supported by extra resource materials.

The **introductory lesson** introduces students to background information about places, people, and events mentioned throughout this novel. It also doubles as the first writing assignment for the unit. Following the introductory activity, students are given an explanation of how the activity relates to the book they are about to read. The next lesson following the transition, students are given the materials they will be using during the unit.

The **reading assignments** are approximately twenty-five pages each; some are a little shorter while others are a little longer. Students have approximately 15 minutes of pre-reading work to do prior to each reading assignment. This pre-reading work involves reviewing the study questions for the assignment and doing some vocabulary work for the vocabulary words they will encounter in their reading.

The **study guide questions** are fact-based questions; students can find the answers to these questions right in the text. These questions come in two formats: short answer or multiple choice The best use of these materials is probably to use the short answer version of the questions as study guides for students (since answers will be more complete), and to use the multiple choice version for occasional quizzes. It might be a good idea to make transparencies of your answer keys for the overhead projector.

The **vocabulary work** is intended to enrich students' vocabularies as well as to aid in the students' understanding of the book. Prior to each reading assignment, students will complete a two-part worksheet for the vocabulary words in the upcoming reading assignment. Part I focuses on students' use of general knowledge and contextual clues by giving the sentence in which the word appears in the text. Students are then to write down what they think the words mean based on the words' usage. Part II nails down the definitions of the words by giving students dictionary definitions of the words and having students match the words to the correct definitions based on the words' contextual usage. Students should then have an understanding of the words when they meet them in the text.

After each reading assignment, students will go back and formulate answers for the study guide questions. Discussion of these questions serves as a **review** of the most important events and ideas presented in the reading assignments.

After students complete extra discussion questions, there is a **vocabulary review** lesson which pulls together all of the fragmented vocabulary lists for the reading assignments and gives students a review of all of the words they have studied.

Following the reading of the book, two lessons are devoted to the **extra discussion questions/writing assignments**. These questions focus on interpretation, critical analysis and personal response, employing a variety of thinking skills and adding to the students' understanding of the novel. These questions are done as a **group activity**. Using the information they have acquired so far through individual work and class discussions, students get together to further examine the text and to brainstorm ideas relating to the themes of the novel.

The group activity is followed by a **reports and discussion** session in which the groups share their ideas about the book with the entire class; thus, the entire class gets exposed to many different ideas regarding the themes and events of the book.

There are three **writing assignments** in this unit, each with the purpose of informing, persuading, or having students express personal opinions. The first assignment is to inform: students will write a composition about one of the background topics assigned in Lesson One. The second assignment is to give students a chance to persuade: students pretend to be a frustrated Annie writing to Mr. Anagnos of The Perkin's Institute asking him to allow her to return and give her a teaching job there. The third assignment gives students the opportunity to express their personal ideas: students will share a time they taught someone something meaningful.

In addition, there is a **nonfiction reading assignment**. Students are required to read a piece of nonfiction related in some way to *The Miracle Worker*. After reading their nonfiction pieces, students will fill out a worksheet on which they answer questions regarding facts, interpretation, criticism, and personal opinions. During one class period, students make **oral presentations** about the nonfiction pieces they have read. This not only exposes all students to a wealth of information, it also gives students the opportunity to practice **public speaking**.

There is an optional **class project** (Seeing and Hearing Through Your Hands) through which students gain first-hand knowledge of and utilize Braille and sign language.

The **review lesson** pulls together all of the aspects of the unit. The teacher is given four or five choices of activities or games to use which all serve the same basic function of reviewing all of the information presented in the unit.

The **unit test** comes in two formats: all multiple choice-matching-true/false or with a mixture of matching, short answer, and composition. As a convenience, two different tests for each format have been included.

There are additional **support materials** included with this unit. The **unit resource section** includes suggestions for an in-class library, crossword and word search puzzles related to the novel, and extra vocabulary worksheets. There is a list of **bulletin board ideas** which gives the teacher suggestions for bulletin boards to go along with this unit. In addition, there is a list of **extra class activities** the teacher could choose from to enhance the unit or as a substitution for an exercise the teacher might feel is inappropriate for his/her class. **Answer keys** are located directly after the **reproducible student materials** throughout the unit. The student materials may be reproduced for use in the teacher's classroom without infringement of copyrights. No other portion of this unit may be reproduced without the written consent of Teacher's Pet Publications, Inc.

UNIT OBJECTIVES - *The Miracle Worker*

1. Through reading William Gibson's, *The Miracle Worker*, students will gain a better understanding of the themes of courage, patience, and perseverence.

2. Students will demonstrate their understanding of the text on four levels: factual, interpretive, critical and personal.

3. Students will define their own viewpoints on the aforementioned themes.

4. Students will be exposed to the post-Civil War era in the South.

5. Students will become familiar with and use Braille and Sign Language.

6. Students will be given the opportunity to practice reading aloud and silently to improve their skills in each area.

7. Students will answer questions to demonstrate their knowledge and understanding of the main events and characters in *The Miracle Worker* as they relate to the author's theme development.

8. Students will enrich their vocabularies and improve their understanding of the novel through the vocabulary lessons prepared for use in conjunction with the novel.

9. The writing assignments in this unit are geared to several purposes:
    a. To have students demonstrate their abilities to inform, to persuade, or to express their own personal ideas
        Note: Students will demonstrate ability to write effectively to <u>inform</u> by developing and organizing facts to convey information. Students will demonstrate the ability to write effectively to <u>persuade</u> by selecting and organizing relevant information, establishing an argumentative purpose, and by designing an appropriate strategy for an identified audience. Students will demonstrate the ability to write effectively to <u>express personal ideas</u> by selecting a form and its appropriate elements.
    b. To check the students' reading comprehension
    c. To make students think about the ideas presented by the novel
    d. To encourage logical thinking
    e. To provide an opportunity to practice good grammar and improve students' use of the English language.

READING ASSIGNMENT SHEET - *The Miracle Worker*

Date Assigned	Reading Assignment	Completion Date
	Act I (pages 1- *top* 23)	
	Act I (pages *mid* 23 - 47)	
	Act II (pages 48 - *top* 71)	
	Act II (pages *mid* 71 -91)	
	Act III (pages 92 - *top* 107)	
	Act III (pages *mid* 107-122)	

Note: Since *The Miracle Worker* is a play, it is really meant to be acted-out on the stage. If you and your students are so inclined and interested, a production with minimal props is possible. This unit is not planned for complete production. However, it is planned to have the parts spoken by various students during in-class reading. A list of characters needed for reading is provided, and a group reading practice is allowed for in Lesson Three.

UNIT OUTLINE - *The Miracle Worker*

1	2	3	4	5
Library Nonfiction Rdg Assignment Writing Assignment #1	Introduction Role Play Materials	Part Assignments PV Act I Pages 1-23	Read Act I Pages 1-23 PV Act I Pages 23-47	Read Act I Pages 23-47 Characterization
6 Act I Study ?'s & Vocabulary Practice PV Act II Pages 48-71	**7** Read Act II Pages 48-71 Oral Rdg Evaluation	**8** Writing Assignment #2 PV Act II Pages 71-91	**9** Read Act II Pages 71-91	**10** Act II Study ?'s and Vocabulary Practice
11 Writing Evaluation PV Act III Pages 92-107	**12** Read Act III Pages 92-107 PV Act III Pages 107-122	**13** Read Act III Pages 107-122	**14** Act III Study ?'s and Vocabulary Review and Practice	**15** Writing Assignment #3
16 Extra Discussion Questions	**17** Extra Discussion Questions	**18** Vocabulary Review	**19** Unit Review	**20** Test
21 Seeing and Hearing Through Your Hands	**22** Seeing and Hearing Through Your Hands	**23** Seeing and Hearing Through Your Hands		

Key: **P** = Preview Study Questions   **V** = Vocabulary Work   **R** = Reading

STUDY GUIDE QUESTIONS

SHORT ANSWER STUDY GUIDE QUESTIONS - *The Miracle Worker*

Act I Pages 1-23
1. How does Kate discover her baby is blind and deaf?
2. Tell the number of years that elapse between Helen's infancy and the paper doll scene with Percy and Martha.
3. What does Helen do that shows she knows Percy is talking?
4. When Martha removes Helen's hands from her biting mouth, how does she react?
5. To which family member does Helen seem closest?
6. Why is Helen troubled by Aunt Ev's towel doll? How does she remedy the situation?
7. How does the family compensate for Helen's affliction?
8. When does Captain Keller agree to contact the oculist in Baltimore?
9. Helen's half-brother, James, holds what opinion of her?
10. List three pieces of information we learn from Mr. Anagnos' farewell conversation with Annie Sullivan at the Perkins Institute.
11. Name the going away presents Annie receives from Anagnos and the blind girls at the Perkins Institute.

Act I Pages 23-47
1. What gesture does Annie use to indicate her mother?
2. How many treats does Helen secretly receive before dinner? Given by whom?
3. How do we know Helen is aware something different is about to happen?
4. What three advantages does Annie tell Kate she has over another governess?
5. Tell Annie's response to Kate's question, "What will you try to teach her first?"
6. Does Kate like Annie at their first meeting?
7. How does Helen first respond to Annie Sullivan?
8. What word does Annie sign to Helen first? Why?
9. Why has Captain Keller become upset before dinner the day of Annie's arrival?
10. For what reason does James fetch a ladder?
11. Describe Annie's reaction to Helen spitting the hidden key out of her mouth and hiding it in the well.

Act II Pages 48-71
1. What does Annie feel is her greatest obstacle with Helen?
2. Why does Annie have Helen feel the different expressions on her face?
3. How does Kate respond when Annie questions her for rewarding Helen for stabbing her with the needle?
4. For what reason does Annie insist everyone leave the dining room during breakfast?
5. Explain why before exiting the dining room James says to Annie, "If it takes all summer, general"?

Miracle Worker Short Answer Study Questions Page 2

6. Tell Kate's response to the Captain's demand that she tell Annie to change her tactics with Helen or leave.
7. What happens after Annie finally gets Helen to take a spoonful of food from her plate into her mouth?
8. What does Aunt Ev remind Kate of after Annie chases them all out of the dining room?
9. Describe Annie's report to Kate after her ordeal with Helen and her response.
10. Dismayed, what does Annie reread from the Perkin's report upon going to her room?
11. Whose voices does Annie hear in her mind after reviewing the report?

Act II pages 71-91
1. What is Captain Keller's reaction to Annie's work with Helen?
2. What does Annie think is Helen's worst handicap?
3. When Kate shares her fear of sending Helen to an asylum, what do we learn about Annie's past?
4. For what does Annie request from the Kellers if she is to stay on there with them?
5. In what way does Annie respond to James' warning that she ought to just accept Helen's condition?
6. How does the family manage to confuse Helen into thinking she has been taken to some other place and town?
7. Where have they actually taken her?
8. Helen responds in what manner to her new surroundings?
9. Of what use is Percy to Annie the first night alone with Helen?
10. How is Annie feeling at the end of Act II?

Act III Pages 92-107
1. How does Annie think Helen can come out of her shell, like the chick?
2. What has been James' feeling about the two weeks Helen has been gone?
3. In what matter does Kate advise James?
4. What is wrong with Helen's eighteen nouns and three verbs?
5. Annie compares words to what?
6. Does Annie agree with Captain Keller's compliment that Helen's cleanliness is next to Godliness?
7. Annie wants words to take the place of what for Helen?
8. What does Annie ask of Captain and Mrs. Keller?
9. How does Annie feel upon Helen's return to the main house?

Act III Pages 107-122
1. Annie defines obedience without understanding as what?
2. What does she ask of Captain Keller when he compliments her on what she has done with Helen in two short weeks?
3. What greeting does James extend to Annie?

Miracle Worker Short Answer Study Questions Page 3

4. How does Helen behave during her special 'welcome home' dinner?
5. All but whom want to allow Helen her tantrum because, after all, she *is* the guest of honor?
6. Which family members finally agree that the right thing is to allow Annie to take over?
7. Where does Annie take Helen when she removes her from the table? What happens there?
8. What does Helen do next?
9. How do her parents react to this turn of events?
10. What object does Helen offer to Annie?
11. What does Annie sign and whisper to Helen that shows she can now move ahead in her own life?

ANSWERS TO SHORT ANSWER STUDY GUIDE QUESTIONS - *The Miracle Worker*

Act I Pages 1-23

1. How does Kate discover her baby is blind and deaf?
   When Kate passes her hand before Helen's eyes and snaps her fingers, there is no response. She then calls out directly at her ears and again there is no response from the baby.

2. Tell the number of years that elapse between Helen's infancy and the paper doll scene with Percy and Martha.
   Five years have elapsed between these scenes.

3. What does Helen do that shows she knows Percy is talking?
   She sticks her fingers in his mouth and feels his tongue as it is moving.

4. When Martha removes Helen's hands from her biting mouth, how does she react?
   Helen topples Martha to the ground takes the scissors out of her hand.

5. To which family member does Helen seem closest?
   Kate is the first to respond to Helen's needs. She often refers to Helen as "my Helen."

6. Why is Helen troubled by Aunt Ev's towel doll? How does she remedy the situation?
   The dolls has no eyes. She rips two buttons from Aunt Ev's dress and insists they be sewn on for eyes.

7. How does the family compensate for Helen's affliction?
   They allow her to do as she pleases despite the havoc it wreaks.

8. When does Captain Keller agree to contact the oculist in Baltimore?
   After Helen overturns baby Mildred's crib and she is trying to communicate with her mother in an inarticulate manner, he finally agrees to contact Dr. Chisholm.

9. Helen's half-brother, James, holds what opinion of her?
   He thinks she should be put in an asylum.

10. List three pieces of information we learn from Mr. Anagnos' farewell conversation with Annie Sullivan at the Perkins Institute.
    We learn that Annie has a painful past, that she is a strong-willed young woman, and that she has no other offers.

11. Name the going away presents Annie receives from Anagnos and the blind girls at the Perkins Institute.
    Mr. Anagnos gives Annie a loan for her train fare and a garnet ring. The girls give her smoked glasses, to protect her sensitive eyes, and a doll for Helen.

Act I Pages 23-47

1. What gesture does Helen use to indicate her mother ?
    She touches her cheek to indicate her wants.

2. How many treats does Helen secretly receive before dinner? Given by whom?
    She receives three before dinner treats. One from her mother before she leaves to pick up Annie at the train station, one from the Negro servant, Viney, when Anne touches her cheek, and one from her father, whom she kicks in the leg when he tries to take it away.

3. How do we know Helen is aware something different is about to happen?
    She has been smelling and feeling around in the room the Kellers have prepared for Annie.

4. What three advantages does Annie tell Kate she has over another governess?
    When Kate is dismayed at Annie's youth, she tells Kate that she has Dr. Howe's work behind her, she is young and energetic, and that she has been blind.

5. Tell Annie's response to Kate's question , "What will you try to teach her first?"
    She tells Kate that it will be language, for language is to the mind more than light is to the eye.

6. Does Kate like Annie at first?
    Yes, she is amused and impressed with her responses.

7. How does Helen first respond to Annie Sullivan?
    Helen boldly feels her arms and her face and then she drags Annie's suitcase up the stairs to her prepared room.

8. What word does Annie sign to Helen first? Why?
    She first signs the word doll to accompany the new doll the girls have sent for her.

9. Why has Captain Keller become upset before dinner the day of Annie's arrival?
    Annie is locked in her room by Helen who has taken off with the only key.

10. For what reason does James fetch a ladder?
    He gets the ladder to bring Annie down from her locked room through the window.

11. Describe Annie's reaction to Helen spitting the hidden key out of her mouth and hiding it in the well.
    Annie is amused and challenged by Helen's apparent intelligence and guile.

Act II Pages 48-71

1. What does Annie feel is her greatest obstacle with Helen?
    She feels her greatest problem is how to discipline her without breaking her spirit.

2. Why does Annie have Helen feel the different expressions on her face?
    She wants her to associate the expressions and behavior with the words she signs.

3. How does Kate respond when Annie questions her for rewarding Helen for stabbing her with the needle?
    Kate claims that they prefer to catch their flies with honey and regrets that they don't have the heart for much else.

4. For what reason does Annie insist everyone leave the dining room during breakfast?
    She insists they leave so she can try to train Helen uninterrupted by earlier habits allowed by the family.

5. Explain why before exiting the dining room James says to Annie, "If it takes all summer, general"?
    He is taunting her. He and his father had just been having a heated discussion about the battle of Vicksburg in the Civil War.

6. Tell Kate's response to the Captain's demand that she tell Annie to change her tactics with Helen or leave?
    She asks him where will he be when she must tell Annie these things.

7. What happens after Annie finally gets Helen to take a spoonful of food from her plate into her mouth?
    Helen spits it out at Annie and Annie dashes the water from the pitcher into Helen's face.

8. What does Aunt Ev remind Kate of after Annie chases them all out of the dining room?
    She reminds Kate that the child is a Keller, a cousin to Robert E. Lee and that Annie is an unknown.

9. Describe Annie's report to Kate after her ordeal with Helen and Kate's response.
    Worse for the wear, Annie flatly informs her that the room is a wreck, but Helen ate from her own plate and folded her napkin. Kate is beside herself with emotion.

10. Dismayed from her ordeal, what does Annie reread from the Perkin's report upon going to her room?

   She picks up the battered Perkin's report in which patience is encouraged in dealing with a deaf, blind woman. It compares the woman's plight with that of a woman sealed in a caved-in pit. All would bravely dig and dig until the woman in the pit was found and helped.

11. Whose voices does Annie hear in her mind after reviewing the report?

   She hears the voices of her brother, the old crones, and the doctor from the asylum.

Act II Pages 71-91

1. What is Captain Keller's reaction to Annie's work with Helen?

   He is furious with her and has all intentions of firing her.

2. What does Annie think is Helen's worst handicap?

   She feels the family's love and pity is Helen's worst handicap.

3. When Kate shares her fear of sending Helen to an asylum, what do we learn about Annie's past?

   She shares that she grew up in such a place. She tells of the horrors and of her dead brother, Jimmy. She says it made her strong, but that Helen is strong enough already.

4. For what does Annie request from the Kellers if she is to stay on there with them?

   She informs them that Helen needs to be dependent upon her for everything in order for her to teach her. She wants to be isolated with Helen for awhile.

5. In what way does Annie respond to James' warning that she ought to just accept Helen's condition?

   Her idea of giving up is that it was the original sin.

6. How does the family manage to confuse Helen into thinking she has been taken to some other place and town?

   They rode her out in the country in the horse-drawn carriage for two hours.

7. Where have they actually taken her?

   They have simply taken her to their garden house.

8. Helen responds in what manner to her new surroundings?

   She is a' little tornado incarnate'. She is very mad and then breaks down in tears.

9. Of what use is Percy to Annie the first night alone with Helen?

   Since Annie will not touch Annie, she uses Percy as a familiar person to bridge the gap. Annie spells milk into Percy's hand, pushing Helen's curious hand away. Helen then wants Annie to spell only to her.

10. How is Annie feeling at the end of Act II?
    Annie is happy that she has reestablished touch with Helen and sings a lullaby to Helen's baby doll in the moonlight. The other members of the cast seemingly hear her and think of them in the garden house.

Act III Pages 92-107
1. How does Annie think Helen can come out of her shell, like the chick?
    By learning that her fingers can talk.

2. What has been James' feeling about the two weeks Helen has been gone?
    He has enjoyed the quiet and normalcy that has been present.

3. In what matter does Kate advise James?
    She tells him to stand up to the world, including his father.

4. What is wrong with Helen's eighteen nouns and three verbs?
    Annie is exasperated because they are just a finger-game to her with no meaning.

5. Annie compares words to what?
    She tells Kate that we're born to use words like a bird uses wings.

6. Does Annie agree with Captain Keller's compliment that Helen's cleanliness is next to Godliness?
    No, she says it is next to nothing, Helen must learn that everything has a name.

7. Annie wants words to take the place of what for Helen?
    She wants words to be her eyes to everything in the world.

8. What does Annie ask of Captain and Mrs. Keller?
    She asks for more time with Helen alone.

9. How does Annie feel upon Helen's return to the main house?
    She feels like a defeated general on a deserted battlefield.

Act III Pages 107-122
1. Annie defines obedience without understanding as what?
    She says obedience without understanding is a blindness, too.

2. What does she ask of Captain Keller when he compliments her on what she has done with Helen in two short weeks?
    She asks him to stand between Helen and the lie that she can always have her own way.

3. What greeting does James extend to Annie?
    He greets her with, "Evening, general."

4. How does Helen behave during her special 'welcome home' dinner?
    She reverts back to the same behavior she used when eating with her family earlier.

5. All but whom want to allow Helen her tantrum because, after all, she *is* the guest of honor?
    The family wants to carry on as usual, but Annie wants to intervene.

6. Which family members finally agree that the right thing is to allow Annie to take over?
    Kate and James support Annie's efforts opposing Keller and Aunt Ev.

7. Where does Annie take Helen when she removes her from the table? What happens there?
    Annie wants Helens to refill the pitcher at the pump. This is where the miracle happens. Helen comprehends that the water she feels and the fingering Annie is doing are the same thing. She utters the sounds she could speak at six months, wah-wah.

8. What does Helen do next?
    She touches familiar objects and turns to Annie for their spellings including her parents.

9. How do her parents react to this turn of events?
    They are stunned and overcome with emotion. Helen signs the word 'teacher' in Kate's palm and Kate sends her to Annie.

10. What object does Helen offer to Annie?
    She surrenders the keys she asked her mother for to Annie.

11. What does Annie sign and whisper to Helen that shows she can now move ahead in her own life?
    Annie signs and whispers I, love, Helen, forever, and ever. She no longer hears the voices from her past.

MULTIPLE CHOICE STUDY/QUIZ QUESTIONS - *Miracle Worker*

Act I Pages 1-23

1. Kate discovers her baby is blind and deaf when
    a. the doctor announces the diagnosis.
    b. she passes her hand before the baby's eyes and there is no movement.
    c. she shouts directly at her and the baby does not react.
    d. both b and c

2. How many years elapse between Helen's infancy and the paper doll scene with Percy and Martha?
    a. two years
    b. five years
    c. eight years
    d. three years

3. When Percy is talking, Helen keeps
    a. slapping him in the face.
    b. feeling his face as he speaks.
    c. trying to cut up his paper dolls.
    d. sticking her fingers in his mouth feeling his tongue move.

4. When Martha removes Helen's hands from her biting mouth
    a. Helen runs after her to the house.
    b. Helen grabs her set of paper dolls and cuts them into pieces.
    c. Helen topples Martha to the ground takes the scissors out of her hand.
    d. none of the above

5. Which family member seems to be the closest to Helen?
    a. Kate
    b. James
    c. Captain Keller
    d. all of the above

6. Aunt Ev's towel doll
    a. needs her hair braided.
    b. has no eyes.
    c. looks like Helen.
    d. is a special doll made for Martha.

Study Guide/Quiz Questions- *The Miracle Worker* Multiple Choice Format Page 2

7. The Keller family compensates for Helen's affliction by allowing her to do as she pleases.
    a. true
    b. false

8. Captain Keller refuses to agree to contact the oculist in Baltimore.
    a. false
    b. true

9. Helen's half-brother, James Keller, thinks
    a. Helen should be put in an asylum.
    b. Helen is an eyesore.
    c. Helen is to pitied.
    d. all of the above

10. Select the one piece of information we do *not* learn from Mr. Anagnos' farewell conversation with Annie Sullivan at the Perkins Institute.
    a. Annie has no other offers other than the Kellers.
    b. Annie is a strong-willed young woman.
    c. Annie and her brother played with rats in the almshouse.
    d. Annie has a painful past.

11. Name the going away present Annie receives from Anagnos upon leaving the Institute.
    a. doll with movable eyelids
    b. smoked glasses
    c. garnet ring
    d. train fare

Study Guide/Quiz Questions- *The Miracle Worker* Multiple Choice Format Page 3

Act I Pages 23-47

1. How does Helen indicate she wants her mother?
    a. She touches her cheek.
    b. She grunts and pounds on the floor.
    c. She rings the bell on the porch.
    d. None of the above

2. Which Ivy Green resident does *not* give Helen a secret before-dinner treat the day Annie is picked up at the train station?
    a. Kate
    b. Captain Keller
    c. Viney
    d. James

3. Helen is aware something different is about to happen because
    a. Kate has been giving her more attention.
    b. She has been smelling and feeling around in the newly prepared room.
    c. Percy and Martha have been scarce.
    d. All of the above

4. Which of the following is *not* an advantage Annie tells Kate she has over another governess?
    a. She has been blind.
    b. She has lived in an asylum.
    c. She has Dr. Howe's work behind her.
    d. She is young and energetic.

5. How does Annie's respond to Kate's question, "What will you try to teach her first?"
    a. It will be language, for language is to the mind more than light is to the eye.
    b. It will be love, for all important is learned through love.
    c. It will be obedience, for nothing can be gained without discipline.
    d. It will be repetition, because it is the pathway for learning.

6. Kate likes Annie from the first meeting.
    a. false
    b. true

Study Guide/Quiz Questions- *The Miracle Worker* Multiple Choice Format Page 4

7. Helen first responds to Annie Sullivan by
    a. boldly feeling her arms and her face.
    b. dragging Annie's suitcase up the stairs to her prepared room.
    c. ignoring her and retreating to the pump.
    d. grabbing the doll and hugging it tightly.

8. Annie's first word to sign to Helen is her name.
    a. true
    b. false

9. Captain Keller becomes upset before dinner the day of Annie's arrival because
    a. Annie is locked in her room by Helen who has taken off with the only key.
    b. Annie has spoken offensively to him from the minute she stepped out of the carriage.
    c. Annie is not what he expected in a governess.
    d. he is hungry and tired of waiting for dinner.

10. James fetches a ladder
    a. to hang the new lantern on the lamppost.
    b. to retrieve Helen's doll from the roof where she threw it.
    c. to bring Annie down from her locked room through the window.
    d. none of the above

11. Annie's reaction to Helen spitting the key out of her mouth and hiding it in the well is one of which
    a. she is noticeably upset and considering leaving before she unpacks.
    b. she is terrified that Helen will swallow it and choke.
    c. she is amused and challenged by Helen's apparent intelligence and guile.
    d. she has no patience for such behavior.

Study Guide/Quiz Questions- *The Miracle Worker* Multiple Choice Format Page 5

Act II Pages 48-71

1. Annie feels her greatest obstacle with Helen is
    a. how to get Helen to trust her.
    b. how to rid her of all of her earlier learned habits.
    c. how to discipline her without breaking her spirit.
    d. how to get Helen to behave properly at the dinner table.

2. Annie has Helen feel the different expressions on her face to
    a. get Helen to move her doll's mouth to match the expression.
    b. associate the expressions and behavior with the words she signs.
    c. show Helen that it is normal to make different expressions.
    d. indicate the expression of different feelings to Helen.

3. How does Kate respond when Annie questions her for rewarding Helen for stabbing her with the needle?
    a. She claims that they prefer to catch their flies with honey.
    b. She regrets that they don't have the heart for much else.
    c. She says Helen simply cannot be compelled at times.
    d. all of the above

4. Annie insists everyone leave the dining room during breakfast
    a. because she needs time alone with Helen to get to know her eating style.
    b. for her to teach Helen a prayer of grace using sign language.
    c. to allow her time to get the feel of the room she will be dining in for the next week.
    d. so she can try to train Helen uninterrupted by the family.

5. James says to Annie before leaving the dining room, "If it takes all summer, Sergeant"?
    a. true
    b. false

6. What question does Kate ask Captain Keller when he demands that she tell Annie to change her tactics with Helen or leave?
    a. Why must I tell her?
    b. Why don't you tell her?
    c. Where will you be?
    d. None of the above

Study Guide/Quiz Questions- *The Miracle Worker* Multiple Choice Format Page 6

7. When Annie finally gets Helen to take a spoonful of food from her plate into her mouth
    a. Helen spits it out at Annie
    b. Annie dashes the water from the pitcher into Helen's face.
    c. Helen smiles from pride at her accomplishment.
    d. Both a and b

8. After Annie chases them all out of the dining room, Aunt Ev reminds Kate
    a. that Helen is a cousin of Robert E. Lee's.
    b. the governess is not suitable.
    c. she must not pay Annie as much as she had planned.
    d. to fill up the water pitcher that Helen broke.

9. Following her ordeal with Helen, Annie reports to Kate that
    a. she can't do the job adequately.
    b. Helen ate from her own plate
    c. Helen folded her napkin.
    d. Both b and c

10. Dismayed from her ordeal, what does Annie reread upon going to her room?
    a. the Perkin's report
    b. a letter from Jimmy
    c. the Bible
    d. her diary

11. Whose voice *doesn't* Annie hear in her mind after reviewing the Perkin's report?
    a. her brother's
    b. the old crones'
    c. the doctor's from the asylum
    d. Anagnos'

Study Guide/Quiz Questions - *The Miracle Worker* Multiple Choice Format Page 7

Act II Pages 71-91

1. Captain Keller's reaction to Annie's work with Helen
    a. is one of fury with her.
    b. is that he has all intentions of firing her.
    c. is one of outrage at her tactics.
    d. all of the above

2. Annie thinks Helen's worst handicap is
    a. her lack of mental abilities.
    b. her stubbornness and curiosity.
    c. her family's love and pity .
    d. her age and gender.

3. Annie grew up in an asylum, but her brother was sent to an orphanage.
    a. true
    b. false

4. Annie requests the Kellers to
    a. take Helen away to Italy where she can learn braille and sign language.
    b. allow Helen to become dependent upon her for everything.
    c. give her two weeks with Helen alone in the garden house.
    d. both b and c

5. Annie tells James that her idea of the original sin is
    a. the way he snoops around all the time.
    b. giving up.
    c. Adam tempting Eve in the garden of Eden.
    d. sending a disabled child to an asylum.

6. The family manages to confuse Helen into thinking she has been taken to some other place and town by
    a. riding her around in the country for two hours.
    b. allowing her to fall asleep in the carriage and then returning home.
    c. sending her to her cousin's house for the night.
    d. taking her to a family picnic and then riding around and around the house awhile.

Study Guide/Quiz Questions- *The Miracle Worker* Multiple Choice Format Page 8

7. They actually have taken her to
    a. an abandoned estate nearby where Annie has set up house for the two of them.
    b. Aunt Ev's lovely home near the Tennessee border.
    c. the garden house on their own estate, Ivy Green.
    d. a neighbor's unused summer home.

8. What is 'a little tornado incarnate'?
    a. The inclement weather approaching the Alabama plains.
    b. Helen's reaction to her new surroundings.
    c. Annie's reaction to the Captain's criticism of her tactics with Helen.
    d. Helen's half-brother, James,' reaction to Captain Keller's agreement with Annie.

9. Annie uses what two things to get through to Helen the first night?
    a. cake and Helen's jealousy
    b. Helen's curiosity and Percy
    c. milk and cookies
    d. cake and Helen's curiosity

10. At the end of Act II Annie
    a. feels that she has forged a beginning for the two of them.
    b. is happy and hopeful.
    c. wonders what the two weeks will bring.
    d. all of the above

Study Guide/Quiz Questions- *The Miracle Worker* Multiple Choice Format Page 9

Act III Pages 92-107

1. Annie thinks Helen can come out of her shell, like the chick by
    a. trying to understand that she is an intelligent little girl.
    b. learning that her new manners will impress her family.
    c. showing some affection to her teacher.
    d. learning that her fingers can talk.

2. During the two weeks Helen has been gone, James
    a. has learned how to communicate with his father.
    b. has enjoyed the quiet and normalcy that has been present.
    c. read up on the Spanish monks who invented sign language.

3. Kate advises James to
    a. fall in love, get married, and have children to understand parenthood.
    b. stay out of her way when it comes to Helen and to treat Annie much better
    c. stand up to the world, including his father.
    d. learn to be his father's friend, as well as son.

4. Helen's eighteen nouns and three verbs
    a. are just a finger-game to her with no meaning.
    b. come to her very easily.
    c. were learned in three days and five hours.

5. Complete the analogy. Wings are to birds as words are to
    a. meaning
    b. humans
    c. vocal chords

6. Annie agrees with Keller's compliment that Helen's cleanliness is next to Godliness.
    a. true
    b. false

7. What does Annie want to be Helen's eyes to everything in the world?
    a. sign language
    b. herself
    c. words

Study Guide/Quiz Questions- *The Miracle Worker* Multiple Choice Format Page 10

8. Annie asks for more time alone with Helen from Captain and Mrs. Keller.
    a. false
    b. true

9. Upon Helen's return to the main house, Annie feels like
    a. a defeated general on a deserted battlefield.
    b. a victorious Robert E. Lee.
    c. a wounded Confederate soldier at Gettysburg.

Study Guide/Quiz Questions- *The Miracle Worker* Multiple Choice Format Page 11

Act III Pages 107-122

1. Complete Annie's definition for obedience without understanding.
    a. helplessness
    b. blindness
    c. emptiness
    d. carelessness

2. Captain asks Annie to stand between the lie, that she can always have her own way, and Helen.
    a. true
    b. false

3. James greets Annie's return with
    a. nonchalance
    b. annoyance
    c. laughter
    d. none of the above

4. Helen behaves remarkably well during her special 'welcome home' dinner.
    a. true
    b. false

5. All but whom want to allow Helen her tantrum because, after all, she *is* the guest of honor?
    a. Kate
    b. Annie
    c. Keller
    d. Aunt Ev

6. Which two family members finally agree that the right thing is to allow Annie to take over?
    a. Kate and James
    b. James and Keller
    c. Aunt Ev and Kate
    d. Keller and Aunt Ev

7. Helen is taken where by Annie when she is removed from the table? What happens there?
    a. She is dragged downstairs and taken outside to the pump.
    b. Helen utters wah-wah outside at the pump.
    c. Helen associates the singing of the word water with water at the pump.
    d. A miracle takes place outside at the pump.
    e. All of the above

Study Guide/Quiz Questions- *The Miracle Worker* Multiple Choice Format Page 12

8. Select the one below that Helen *does not* do next.
    a. Helen touches familiar objects and wants Annie to sign them to her.
    b. She gets the keys from her mother.
    c. She kicks her father in the leg
    d. Helen signs the word teacher to her mother.

9. The Captain and Kate
    a. are stunned and overcome with emotion.
    b. run to Annie and embrace her.
    c. turn to James and invite him to join them in their reunion with Helen.
    d. None of the above

10. After the breakthrough, Helen offers to Annie
    a. the doll she gave her and signs the word doll.
    b. the water pitcher she came to fill at the pump.
    c. the keys she asked her mother for to Annie.
    d. all of her newly crocheted strings from their two weeks alone.

11. Annie can now move ahead in her own life because she
    a. has learned to love again after her brother's death.
    b. has accomplished what she set out to do with Helen.
    c. has impressed a Civil War Captain and his wife.
    d. has taught Helen that words have meaning.

ANSWER KEY - MULTIPLE CHOICE STUDY/QUIZ QUESTIONS
The Miracle Worker

Act I pgs 1-23
1. D
2. B
3. D
4. C
5. A
6. B
7. A
8. A
9. D
10. C
11. C

Act I pgs 23-47
1. A
2. D
3. B
4. B
5. A
6. B
7. A
8. B
9. A
10. C
11. C

Act II pgs 48-71
1. C
2. B
3. D
4. D
5. B
6. C
7. D
8. A
9. D
10. A
11. D

Act II pgs 71-91
1. D
2. C
3. B
4. D
5. B
6. A
7. C
8. B
9. B
10. D

Act III pgs 92-107
1. D
2. B
3. C
4. A
5. B
6. B
7. C
8. B
9. A

Act III pgs 107-122
1. B
2. B
3. D
4. B
5. B
6. A
7. E
8. C
9. A
10. C

PREREADING VOCABULARY WORKSHEETS

Vocabulary- *The Miracle Worker* Act I Pages 1-12 (Set 1)

Part I: Using Prior Knowledge and Contextual Clues

Below are the sentences in which the vocabulary words appear in the text. Read the sentence. Use any clues you can find in the sentence combined with your prior knowledge, and write what you think the underlined words mean on the lines provided.

1. They have been through a long *vigil* and it shows in their tired bearing and disarranged clothing.
___

2. Doctor (*amiably*): Yes, especially if some of you Kellers don't get a night's sleep. I mean you, Mrs. Keller.
___

3. Keller (*indulgent*): I've brought up two of them, but this is my wife's first, she isn't battle-scarred yet.
___

4. Keller (*jovial*): Put up stronger fencing, ha?
___

5., 6. The third child is Helen, six and a half years old, quite *unkempt*, in body a *vivacious* little person with a fine head, attractive, but noticeably blind.
___

7. Inside, the lights have been gradually coming up on the main room, where we see the family informally gathered, talking, but in *pantomime*.
___

8. A *benign* visitor in a hat, Aunt Ev, is putting the finishing touches on a big shapeless doll made out of towels.
___

9. An *indolent* young man, James Keller, is at the window watching the children.
___

10. James (*blandly*): She only dug Martha's eyes out. Almost dug. It's always almost, no point worrying till it happens, is there?
___

Miracle Worker Vocabulary Set 1 Continued

11. Why, this very famous *oculist* in Baltimore I wrote you about, what was his name?
_____

12. Keller (Rising, *emphatic*): Katie, he can't.
_____

Part II: Determining the Meaning: Match the vocabulary words to their dictionary definitions.

___ 1. vigil   A. pointed; insistent
___ 2. amiably   B. eye doctor
___ 3. indulgent   C. idle; inactive
___ 4. jovial   D. gestures without voice
___ 5. vivacious   E. favorable; pleasant
___ 6. unkempt   F. lively; spirited
___ 7. pantomime   G. jolly; happy
___ 8. benign   H. permissive; lenient
___ 9. indolent   I. flatly; tritely
___ 10. blandly   J. disorderly; messy
___ 11. oculist   K. agreeably; willingly
___ 12. emphatic   L. a watch

Vocabulary- *The Miracle Worker* Act I Pages 12-23 (Set 2)

Part I: Using Prior Knowledge and Contextual Clues
Below are the sentences in which the vocabulary words appear in the text. Read the sentence. Use any clues you can find in the sentence combined with your prior knowledge, and write what you think the underlined words mean on the lines provided.

1. James (*facetiously*): Father stands up, that makes it a fact.
___

2. You be quiet! I'm badgered enough around here by females without your *impudence*.
___

3. James (*placating*): You really ought to put her away, Father.
___

4. I'm as sensible to this *affliction* as anyone else, it hurts me to look at the girl.
___

5. Another kind of silence now, while Kate takes pins and buttons from the sewing basket and attaches them to the doll as eyes. Keller stands, caught, and watches *morosely*.
___

6. But Helen suddenly has come upon the cradle, and hesitatingly overturns it; the *swaddled* baby tumbles out, and Captain Keller barely manages to dive and catch it in time.
___

7. All are in commotion, the baby screams, but Helen *unperturbed* is laying her doll in its place.
___

8. Kate (*inexorably*): Are you willing to put her away?
___

9. The chair contains a girl of 20, Annie Sullivan, with a face which in repose is grave and rather obstinate, and when active is impudent, *combative*, twinkling with all the life that Helen's lacks.
___

10. Her eyes are inflamed, vague, slightly crossed, clouded by the granular growth of *trachoma*.
___

Miracle Worker Vocabulary Set 2 Continued

11. She cannot continue until she finds a <u>*woebegone*</u> joke.
_____

12. We hear a boy's voice whispering; perhaps we see shadowy <u>*intimations*</u> of these speakers in the background.
_____

Part II: Determining the Meaning: Match the vocabulary words to their dictionary definitions.

___ 13. facetiously
___ 14. impudence
___ 15. placating
___ 16. affliction
___ 17. morosely
___ 18. unperturbed
___ 19. swaddled
___ 20. inexorably
___ 21. trachoma
___ 22. combative
___ 23. woebegone
___ 24. intimations

A. satisfying; gratifying
B. sullenly; gloomily
C. unbothered; calm
D. hints; allusions
E. miserable
F. hardship; problem
G. inflammation of the eyelids
H. boldly
I. wrapped up
J. relentlessly; unyielding
K. ready for battle
L. flippant; smart-alecky

Vocabulary- *The Miracle Worker* Act I Pages 23-47 (Set 3)

Part I: Using Prior Knowledge and Contextual Clues
Below are the sentences in which the vocabulary words appear in the text. Read the sentence. Use any clues you can find in the sentence combined with your prior knowledge, and write what you think the underlined words mean on the lines provided.

1. Viney (*reproachfully*): Cap'n Keller, now how'm I gone get her to eat her supper you fill her up with that trash?
   _____

2. Kate is studying her face, and Annie returns the gaze; this is a mutual *appraisal*, southern gentlewoman and working-class Irish girl, and Annie is not quite comfortable under it.
   _____

3., 4. I expected- a *desiccated spinster*. You're very young.
   _____

5. Annie (*resolutely*): Oh, you should have seen me when I left Boston, I got much older on this trip.
   _____

6. Annie takes the bull by the horns, *valiantly*.
   _____

7. Keller (*sotto voce*): Katie--
   _____

8. The first thing Helen pulls out is a *voluminous* shawl. She fingers it till she perceives what it is.
   _____

9. Annie studies her, still in bonnet and smoked glasses, like a *caricature* of herself, and addresses her humorously.
   _____

10. Annie regards her stonily, but Helen after a scowling moment tugs at her hand again, *imperious*.
    _____

11. Helen's hand waits, *baffled*, Annie repeats it.
    _____

Miracle Worker Vocabulary Set 3 Continued

12. Annie takes a handkerchief, nurses her mouth, stands in the middle of the room, staring at the door and window in turn and so catches sight of herself in the mirror, her cheek scratched, her hair *disheveled*, her handkerchief bloody, her face disgusted with herself.

_____

13. Annie (with some *asperity*): Well, if there was a key in here, I wouldn't be in here.

_____

14. Oh no. It's -very *chivalrous* of you, but I'd really prefer to-

_____

15. Annie ignores him, looking at Helen; James goes in too. *Imperceptibly*, the lights commence to narrow down.

_____

Part II: Determining the Meaning: Match the vocabulary words to their dictionary definitions.

___ 25. reproachfully   A. evaluation
___ 26. appraisal   B. unnoticeably; barely
___ 27. desiccated   C. old maid
___ 28. spinster   D. somewhat ill-tempered
___ 29. resolutely   E. gentlemanly; gallant
___ 30. valiantly   F. indistinct, out of earshot
___ 31. sotto voce   G. disapprovingly; critically
___ 32. voluminous   H. bravely. courageously
___ 33. caricature   I. rumpled; untidy
___ 34. imperious   J. confused; bewildered
___ 35. baffled   K. deliberately; willfully
___ 36. disheveled   L. urgent; pressing
___ 37. asperity   M. exaggeration; model
___ 38. chivalrous   N. dried up
___ 39. imperceptibly   O. bulky; large

Vocabulary- *The Miracle Worker* Act II Pages 48-71 (Set 4)

Part I: Using Prior Knowledge and Contextual Clues
Below are the sentences in which the vocabulary words appear in the text. Read the sentence. Use any clues you can find in the sentence combined with your prior knowledge, and write what you think the underlined words mean on the lines provided.

1. All right, let's try *temperance.*

_____

2. Annie leaps to her feet, and stands *inarticulate*; Helen calmly gropes back to sit to the sewing card and needle.

_____

3. Annie reaches for the sewing card, Helen objects, Annie insists, and Helen objects, Annie insists, and Helen gets rid of Annie's hand by jabbing it with the needle; Annie gasps, and moves to grip Helen's wrist; but Kate intervenes with a *proffered* sweet.

_____

4. Annie (indignantly): Why does she get a reward? For stabbing me?

_____

5. We haven't the heart for much else, and so many times she simply cannot be *compelled*.

_____

6. Kate catches Annie's eyes on her, smiles with a wry gesture. Helen moves on to James' plate, the male talk continuing, James *deferential* and Keller overriding.

_____

7. *Obstinate*. Could any of them compare even in that with old Stonewall? If he'd been there we would still have Vicksburg.

_____

8. For this *tyrant*? The whole house turns on her whims, is there anything she wants she doesn't get?

_____

9. Annie closes the door on James, locks it, removes the key, and turns with her back against the door to stare *ominously* at Helen, kicking on the floor.

_____

Miracle Worker Vocabulary Set 4 Continued

10. Helen's next attempt to topple it is *unavailing*, so her fingers dive in a pinch at Annie's flank.
___

11. Annie's hand in *compunction* falters to her own face, but when Helen hits at her again, Annie deliberately slaps her again.
___

12. Helen lifts her fist *irresolute* for another roundhouse, Annie lifts her hand resolute for another slap, and they freeze in this posture, while Helen mulls this over.
___

13. Helen *writhes* out of her chair, runs to the front door, and tugs and kicks at it.
___

14. The pain brings Annie to her knees, and Helen *pummels* her; they roll under the table, and the lights commence to dim out on them.
___

15. Martha shifts Helen's doll in her clutch, and it *plaintively* says momma.
___

Part II Determining the Meaning: Match the vocabulary words to their dictionary definitions.

___ 55. temperance
___ 56. inarticulate
___ 57. proffered
___ 58. indignantly
___ 59. compelled
___ 60. deferential
___ 61. obstinate
___ 62. tyrant
___ 63. ominously
___ 64. unavailing
___ 65. compunction
___ 66. irresolute
___ 67. writhes
___ 68. pummels
___ 69. plaintively

A. thrashes; beats
B. harsh, cruel ruler
C. wordless; silent
D. uncertain; hesitant
E. darkly; gloomily
F. shame; regret
G. hopeless; futile
H. respectful; obedient
I. obliged; made responsible
J. righteously angry
K. moderation
L. offered forth
M. stubborn; headstrong
N. sorrowfully; sadly
O. twists from pain

Vocabulary- *The Miracle Worker* Act II Page 71-91 (Set 5)

Part I: Using Prior Knowledge and Contextual Clues
Below are the sentences in which the vocabulary words appear in the text. Read the sentence. Use any clues you can find in the sentence combined with your prior knowledge, and write what you think the underlined words mean on the lines provided.

1., 2. From the moment she stepped off the train she's been nothing but a burden, incompetent, *impertinent, ineffectual*, immodest-

_____

3. Katie. I did not bring you all the way out here to the garden house to be *frivolous*.

_____

4. Keller (*vexedly*): Miss Sullivan, I find it difficult to talk through those glasses.

_____

5. Keller (*dourly*): Why do you wear them, the sun has been down for an hour.

_____

6. Keller (*nonplussed*): Then- do I understand you- propose-

_____

7. Everything. The food she eats, the clothes she wears, fresh air, yes, the air she breathes, whatever her body needs is a -*primer*, to teach her out of.

_____

8. I grew up in such as asylum. The state's *almshouse*.

_____

9. Annie now drags the box of toys into the center, props up the doll *conspicuously* on top; with the people melted away, except for James, all is again still.

_____

10. James (*nettled*): You won't open her. Why can't you let her be? Have some-pity on her, for being what she is-

_____

11. Helen waits and then *recommences* her groping, more urgently.

_____

Miracle Worker Vocabulary Set 5 Continued

12. When she has covered the room, she commences her weird screaming. Annie moves to comfort her, but her touch sends Helen into a *paroxysm* of rage.
___

13. Helen's hand waits, *intractably* waits.
___

14. Annie whispers to it in mock *solicitude*.
___

15. She lays it on her shoulder, and begins rocking with it, patting its *diminutive* behind; she talks the lullaby to it, humorously at first.
___

Part II: Determining the Meaning: Match the vocabulary words to their dictionary definitions.

___ 55. impertinent	A. concern
___ 56. ineffectual	B. inflexibly; headstrong
___ 57. frivolous	C. repeated; began again
___ 58. vexedly	D. sanitarium
___ 59. dourly	E. drearily
___ 60. nonplussed	F. bothered; peeved
___ 61. primer	G. trivial; petty
___ 62. almshouse	H. rude; impolite
___ 63. conspicuously	I. useless
___ 64. nettled	J. irritatedly
___ 65. recommences	K. manual; handbook
___ 66. paroxysm	L. bewildered; puzzled
___ 67. intractably	M. clearly; obviously
___ 68. solicitude	N. fit; attack
___ 69. diminutive	O. small

Vocabulary- *The Miracle Worker* Act III Pages 92-107 (Set 6)

Part I: Using Prior Knowledge and Contextual Clues
Below are the sentences in which the vocabulary words appear in the text. Read the sentence. Use any clues you can find in the sentence combined with your prior knowledge, and write what you think the underlined words mean on the lines provided.

1. It's true. The two weeks have been normal, quiet, all you say. But not short. *Interminable*.
   _____

2. Annie, *haggard* at the table, is writing a letter, her face almost in contact with the stationery.
   _____

3. Annie twinkles at Kate with mock *devoutness*.
   _____

4. Annie (*withering*): Cleaner.
   _____

5. She makes letters with her fingers, show them to Belle, waits with her palm, then *manipulates* the dog's claws.
   _____

6. Helen with her hand free strokes her cheek, suddenly *forlorn*, Annie takes her hand again.
   _____

7. She turns, gazing around at the stripped room, bidding it silently farewell, *impassively*, like a defeated general on the deserted battlefield.
   _____

Part II: Determining the Meaning: Match the vocabulary words to their dictionary definitions.

___ 70. interminable   A. unemotionally
___ 71. haggard   B. shrinking; shriveling
___ 72. devoutness   C. godliness; piety
___ 73. withering   D. maneuvers; moves
___ 74. manipulates   E. care worn; drawn
___ 75. forlorn   F. unending; ceaseless
___ 76. impassively   G. forsaken; abandoned

Vocabulary- *The Miracle Worker* Act III Pages 107-122 (Set 7)

Part I: Using Prior Knowledge and Contextual Clues
Below are the sentences in which the vocabulary words appear in the text. Read the sentence. Use any clues you can find in the sentence combined with your prior knowledge, and write what you think the underlined words mean on the lines provided.

1. The remaining suggestion of garden house is gone now, and the water pump is *unobstructed*.
___

2. She tries to *disengage* Helen's hand; Kate lays hers on Annie's.
___

3. Helen begins to fight and kick, clutching to the tablecloth, and uttering *laments*.
___

4. It's not unnatural, most of us take *some aversion* to our teachers, and occasionally another hand can smooth things out
___

5. He is starting after Annie when James, on his feet with shaky resolve, *interposes* his chair between him and Keller's path.
___

6. If you drive her away from here it will be over my dead -chair, has it ever occurred to you that on one occasion you might be *consummately* wrong?
___

7. Kate rises in *trepidation*, to mediate.
___

8. Helen drops the pitcher on the slab under the spout, it shatters. She stands *transfixed*.
___

9. Kate comprehends it, their first act of verbal communication, and she can hardly utter the word aloud, in wonder, gratitude, and *deprivation*; it is a moment in which she simultaneously finds and loses a child.
___

Miracle Worker Vocabulary Set 7 Continued

10. Annie turns; and Kate, facing Helen in her direction by the shoulders, holds her back, and then *relinquishes* her.

Part II: Determining the Meaning: Match the vocabulary words to their dictionary definitions.

___ 77. unobstructed
___ 78. disengage
___ 79. aversion
___ 80. laments
___ 81. interposes
___ 82. consummately
___ 83. deprivation
___ 84. relinquishes

A. loss
B. resigns; gives up
C. distaste; dislike
D. absolutely; perfectly
E. in open view
F. release; undo
G. intervenes, interferes
H. moans; wails

ANSWER KEY - VOCABULARY
The Miracle Worker

Set 1	Set 2	Set 3	Set 4	Set 5
1. L	13. L	25. G	40. K	55. H
2. K	14. H	26. A	41. C	56. I
3. H	15. A	27. N	42. L	57. G
4. G	16. F	28. C	43. J	58. J
5. F	17. B	29. K	44. I	59. E
6. J	18. C	30. H	45. H	60. L
7. D	19. I	31. F	46. M	61. K
8. E	20. J	32. O	47. B	62. D
9. C	21. G	33. M	48. E	63. M
10. I	22. K	34. L	49. G	64. F
11. B	23. E	35. J	50. F	65. C
12. A	24. D	36. I	51. D	66. N
		37. D	52. O	67. B
		38. E	53. A	68. A
		39. B	54. N	69. O

Set 6	Set 7
70. F	77. E
71. E	78. F
72. C	79. C
73. B	80. H
74. D	81. G
75. G	82. D
76. A	83. A
	84. B

DAILY LESSONS

LESSON ONE

Objectives
1. To give students background information for *The Miracle Worker*
2. To give students the opportunity to fulfill their nonfiction reading assignment that goes along with this unit
3. To give students practice using library resources
4. To prepare students for the introductory activity in Lesson Two.
5. To give students the opportunity to write to inform by developing and organizing facts to convey information.

Activity

Assign one of each of the following topics to a small group of your students. Distribute Writing Assignment #1. Discuss the directions in detail. Take your students to the library so they may work on the assignment. Students should fill out a "Nonfiction Assignment Sheet" for at least one of the sources they used, and students should submit these sheets with their compositions.

Topics:
1. What is braille? How is it used? How did it come into use?
2. When and who developed sign language?
3. Demonstrate the major symbols used in signing.
4. Who is Helen Keller?
5. During what years did the Civil War take place?
6. What were the main issues of the Civil War?
7. Which side won the Civil War and what did it signify?
8. List the significant battles of the Civil War and their outcomes.
9. Name the most prominent generals for the South and the North in the Civil War.
10. What and where is the Perkin's Institute?
11. How are blind and deaf children able to learn ?
12. What did Alexander Graham Bell have to do with deaf education?
13. Where and what is The Perkins Institute?
14. Where is Radcliffe College? What caliber of educational institution is it?
15. Where is Tuscumbia, Alabama?
16. Of what significance was the Battle of Vicksburg?
17. What would living in a state asylum (almshouse) be like in the 1880's?
18. How has the treatment of and the effects of diseases such as acute congestion changed since the 1880's?
19. What accomplishments did Helen Keller achieve in her lifetime?
20. Who was Robert E. Lee? What did he represent to the South?
21. Who was Polly Thompson?
22. What is the Horace Mann School and where is it located?
23. Who is Dr. Samuel Gridley Howe?
24. Who was Annie Sullivan?

WRITING ASSIGNMENT #1 - *The Miracle Worker*

PROMPT

You are going to read a remarkable play about a blind and deaf five-year-old girl that takes place in the post-Civil War South in the United States during the 1880's. Before you read it, however, it would be beneficial for you to have some background information about some of the people, places, and things mentioned in the story.

You have been assigned one topic about which you must find information. You are to read as much as you can about that topic and write a composition in which you relate what you have learned from your reading. Note that this is a *composition*, not just a sentence or two.

PREWRITING

You will go to the library. When you get there, use the library's resources to find information about your topic. Look for books, encyclopedias, articles in magazines- anything that will give you the information you require. Take a few notes as you read to help you remember important dates, names, places, or other details that will be important in your composition.

After you have gathered information and become well-read on the subject of your report, make a little outline, putting your facts in order.

DRAFTING

You will need an introductory paragraph in which you introduce your topic.

In the body of your composition, put the "meat" of your research- the facts you found- in paragraph form. Each paragraph should have a topic sentence (a sentence letting the reader know what the paragraph will be about) followed by an explanation, examples, or details.

Write a concluding paragraph in which you summarize the information you found and conclude your report.

PROMPT

After you have finished a rough draft of your paper, revise it yourself until you are happy with your work. Then, ask a student who sits near you to tell you what he/she likes best about your work, and what things he/she thinks can be improved. Take another look at your composition, keeping in mind your critic's suggestions, and make the revisions you feel are necessary.

PROOFREADING

Do a final proofreading of your paper double-checking your grammar, spelling, organization, and the clarity of your ideas.

NONFICTION ASSIGNMENT SHEET - *The Miracle Worker*
(To be completed after reading the required nonfiction article)

Name _____ Date _____

Title of Nonfiction Read _____

Written By _____ Publication Date _____

I. Factual Summary: Write a short summary of the piece you read.

II. Vocabulary
    1. With which vocabulary words in the piece did you encounter some degree of difficulty?

    2. How did you resolve your lack of understanding with these words?

III. Interpretation: What was the main point the author wanted you to get from reading his work?

IV. Criticism
    1. With which points of the piece did you agree or find easy to accept? Why?

    2. With which points of the piece did you disagree or find difficult to believe? Why?

V. Personal Response: What do you think about this piece? <u>OR</u> How does this piece influence your ideas?

LESSON TWO

Objectives
    1. To introduce *The Miracle Worker* unit
    2. To check students' nonfiction reading assignments
    3. To assimilate blindness through a simple role play
    4. To distribute books and other materials (study guides, reading assignments, etc.)

Note: Prior to this class please post a large silhouette of a female, perhaps wearing dark glasses.

Activity #1
    Provide students with a small piece of colored paper of their choice. Allow them to make it the shape of something that represents a fact learned from their research (for example: a small Union flag). Have each of them write one fact he/she learned from his/her research on their shape. Students could briefly illustrate their shape, if time allows. Have students one by one, bring their fact up to the silhouette and post it. Encourage placement for an attractive display. Students could also write directly on the bulletin board paper. After they have placed their fact up, have them share. Discuss each fact briefly as it is presented so all students will be exposed to a wide variety of background information before reading. After all have shared, ask students to brainstorm a **name** for their display based on the information generated. Post title.

TRANSITION: After all students have had the opportunity to share, ask them how being blind and deaf would change their life. In pairs, have students blindfold each other. Allow the blindfolded student to try to explore a familiar area for a few minutes. Switch roles. Discuss observations. Tell them tomorrow they will begin the story of how one such young girl overcame two severe disabilities to become a productive member of society.

Activity #2
    Distribute the materials students will use in this unit. Explain in detail how students are to use these materials.

    Study Guides Students should preview the study guide questions before each reading assignment to get a feeling for what events and ideas are important in that section. After reading the section, students will (as a class or individually) answer the questions to review the important events and ideas from that section of the book. Students should keep the study guides as study materials for the unit test.

    Vocabulary Prior to reading a reading assignment, students will do vocabulary work related to the section of the book they are about to read. Following the completion of the reading of the book, there will be a vocabulary review of all the words used in the vocabulary assignments. Students should keep their vocabulary work as study materials for the unit test.

Reading Assignment Sheet You need to fill in the reading assignment sheet to let students know when their reading has to be completed. You can either write the assignment sheet on a side blackboard or bulletin board and leave it there for students to see each day, or you can make copies for each student to have. In either case, you should advise students to become very familiar with the reading assignments so they know what is expected of them.

Extra Activities Center The unit resource portion of this unit contains suggestions for a library of related books and articles in your classroom as well as crossword and word search puzzles. Make an extra activities center in your room where you will keep these materials for students to use. (Bring the books and articles in from the library and keep several copies of the puzzles on hand.) Explain to students that these materials are available for students to use when they finish reading assignments or other class work early

Books Each school has its own rules and regulations regarding student use of school books. Advise students of the procedures that are normal for your school.

LESSON THREE

Objectives
1. To assign students to various parts in the play
2. To familiarize students with the vocabulary in Act I Pages 1-23
3. To familiarize students with the study questions for Act I Pages 1-23
4. To give students time to practice their oral reading assignments

Activity #1
    Have students examine the cover of the book and briefly look through it. Point out the structure of the play. On this and the next page you will find a list of all the speaking and acting parts for each of the reading divisions of *The Miracle Worker*. Assign one part to each of your students. You may want to alternate parts if you have a large class. Also, there is quite a bit of narration, so you may want to assign a number of students to that role.

Activity #2
    Tell students that they have the remainder of this class period to do the prereading work for Act I, which includes completing the vocabulary worksheet and previewing the study questions for the first section of reading (pages 1-23). If they finish early, they should read over and practice the lines in the upcoming oral reading section to which they have been assigned.

PLAY PARTS BY READING SECTIONS - *The Miracle Worker*

Act I Pages 1-23

Narrator	James Keller
Doctor	Aunt Ev
Captain Keller	Michael Anagnos
Kate Keller	Annie Sullivan
Martha	Blind Children
Percy	Beatrice
Helen	Smallest Child
Jimmy Sullivan (Boy's Voice)	Man's Voice

Act I Pages 23-47

Narrator	Annie Sullivan
Viney	Jimmy Sullivan (Boy's Voice)
Captain Keller	First Crone Voice
Kate Keller	Second Crone Voice
James Keller	Third Crone Voice
Helen	Doctor's Voice

Act II Pages 48-71

Narrator	Aunt Ev
Annie Sullivan	Martha
Helen	Man's Voice
Kate Keller	Jimmy Sullivan (Boy's Voice)
Viney	First Crone Voice
Captain Keller	Second Crone Voice
James Keller	Third Crone Voice
	Doctor's Voice

Act II Pages 71-91

Narrator
Annie Sullivan
Helen
Kate Keller
Percy
Captain Keller
James Keller
Jimmy Sullivan (Boy's Voice)

Act III Pages 92-107

Narrator
Annie Sullivan
Helen
Kate Keller
Captain Keller
James Keller
Jimmy Sullivan (Boy's Voice
Anagnos' Voice

Act III Pages 107-122

Narrator
Annie Sullivan
Helen
Kate Keller
Captain Keller
James Keller
Aunt Ev
Viney

LESSON FOUR

Objectives
1. To read Act I pages 1-23
2. To give students practice reading orally
3. To familiarize students with the study questions and vocabulary in Act I pages 23-47

Activity #1

Have students read Act I pages 1-23 of *The Miracle Worker* out loud in class. Model and instruct good reading and speaking skills based on the upcoming oral reading evaluation components (fluency, clarity, audibility, pronunciation, and characterization).

Activity #2

Inform students that prior to the next class session they should complete the upcoming (Act I pages 23-47) vocabulary worksheet and preview the study questions for these pages.

LESSON FIVE

Objectives
1. To read Act I pages 23-47
2. To give students practice reading orally
3. To have students chart characterization for one character from play

Activity # 1

Have students read their assigned parts for this section of reading. Stress characterization based upon earlier exposure to their characters in the first reading section.

Activity # 2

Duplicate characterization chart below on the chalkboard or the overhead. Place one of the character's names in the top of the table. Fill out as a class; guiding student responses based on specific examples of the character's **physical traits, actions, speech, thoughts** or **feelings** and **what others say about that character**. Hand out blank chart to class. Students need to copy the information from this one when you have completed it.

Activity # 3

Divide the class into small groups or pairs, depending on the # of students. Hand out only one chart per group. Have each group assign a recorder. Have groups choose a remaining main character from the play to chart working together reviewing the first Act.

Activity # 4

Have students select a representative from each of their groups to share their group's character chart with the class. Have all students summarize information for all main characters. Each student will need enough copies (use back and front). Be sure students save charts for future use and reference. If time runs out, students may continue during time you are doing writing conferences in another lesson.

CHARACTERIZATION CHART

for _____
     NAME

Physical traits	Actions	Feelings; thoughts	Speech	What others say

LESSON SIX

Objectives
1. To review and practice the study questions and vocabulary from Act I (pages 1-47)
2. To familiarize students with the study questions and vocabulary in Act II pages 48-71
3. To give students time to practice their upcoming oral reading

Activity #1

Discuss the answers to the study questions and vocabulary for Act I in detail. Write the answers on the board or overhead transparency so students can have the correct answers for study purposes. Note: It is a good practice in public speaking and leadership skills for individual students to take charge of leading the discussions of the study questions and vocabulary. Perhaps a different student could go to the front of the class and lead the discussion each day that the study questions are discussed during this unit. Of course, the teacher should guide the discussion when appropriate and be sure to fill in any gaps the students leave.

Activity #2

Have students complete the upcoming (Act II pages 48-71) vocabulary worksheet and preview the study questions for these pages. Allow time for practice reading of these pages for next reading in class.

LESSON SEVEN

Objectives
1. To read Act II pages 48-71
2. To give students practice reading orally
3. To give the teacher the opportunity to evaluate students' oral reading

Activity # 1

Have students read their assigned parts for this section of reading. Fill out the following form for each student as they read their parts. If you do not finish during this reading session complete during Lessons 9, 12, or 13.

ORAL READING EVALUATION - *The Miracle Worker*

Name _____ Class____ Date _____

SKILL	EXCELLENT	GOOD	AVERAGE	FAIR	POOR
Fluency	5	4	3	2	1
Clarity	5	4	3	2	1
Audibility	5	4	3	2	1
Pronunciation	5	4	3	2	1
Characterization	5	4	3	2	1
_____	5	4	3	2	1
_____	5	4	3	2	1

Total _____   Grade _____

Comments:

LESSON EIGHT

<u>Objectives</u>
    1. To give students practice in writing to persuade
    2. To preview vocabulary and main ideas and events from Act II pages 71-91

<u>Activity #1</u>
    Assign PVR for Act II pages 71-91 as homework to be completed by the next class session.

<u>Activity #2</u>
    Distribute Writing Assignment #2 and discuss the directions in detail. Allow the remaining class time for students to complete the assignment. Give them specifics of when final copies are due to you so you have time to review before the writing conferences in Lesson 11.

WRITING ASSIGNMENT #2 - *The Miracle Worker*

PROMPT

At the end of the reading on page 71 Annie has just experienced her first bout with Helen's fury and ill-temperedness. She is greatly disturbed and begins to load her open suitcase with her things from the bureau.

In this writing assignment, pretend you are a frustrated Annie Sullivan wishing to leave the governess job at the Kellers in Alabama. You are ready to return to The Perkin's Institute for the Blind in Boston . Your objective is to write a letter to Mr. Anagnos persuading him to hire you on as a teacher at the institute.

PREWRITING

To begin with, gather support for your viewpoint. Create a list of facts, opinions, and examples that support your point of view. Come up with any and all possible arguments you can think of that will promote your side of this issue. Decide which are your strongest justifiable arguments, and which are less substantial. Organize your points from weaker to strongest utilizing your facts, opinions, and examples as evidence in support of your argument.

DRAFTING

Begin with an introductory paragraph in which you express your discouragement and exhaustion from your recent encounter with Helen in the dining room. Follow that with one paragraph for each of the main points you have to support your argument to convince slave owners to stop slave trading. Fill in each paragraph with your facts, opinions, and examples that support your main point. Then, write an ending paragraph that summarizes and restates your opposition to this practice as your final statement.

PROMPT

When you finish the rough draft of your paper, ask a student who sits near you to read it. After reading your rough draft, he\she should tell you what he\she liked best about your work, which parts were difficult to understand, and ways in which your work could be improved. Reread your paper considering your critic's comments, and make the corrections you think are necessary.

PROOFREADING

Do a final proofreading of your paper double-checking your grammar, spelling, organization, and the clarity of your ideas.

LESSON NINE

Objectives
1. To read Act II pages 48-71
2. To give students practice reading orally
3. To give the teacher the opportunity to evaluate students' oral reading

Activity # 1

Have students read their assigned parts for this section of reading. Continue to fill out an oral reading evaluation form for each student as they read their parts. If you do not finish during this reading session complete during Lessons 12 or 13.

LESSON TEN

Objective

To review and practice the study questions and vocabulary from Act II (pages 48-91)

Activity #1

Hand out four little slips of paper or mini cards to each student that have the letters A,B,C, or D on them. A good idea is to use different color cards for each letter. Use the multiple choice study guide questions and answers on all of Act II for an oral review. Read the question (and/ or show it on the overhead). Then give students the four possible answers, labeling them A, B, C, or D (or show on overhead again). Students respond by holding up the card with what they think is the correct answer. This is one variety of Every Student Response. Remind students not to look at what others are holding up, but to simply display the card of their choice. This is a quick indicator of students' comprehension. You can make it somewhat different by requiring complete silence and having them read the questions silently from the overhead, or make it more mysterious (fun?) by blindfolding everyone and have them hold up a certain number of fingers per answer instead of using the cards.

Activity #2

Have students pair up. Using easels (if available) or scrap/drawing paper, one student draws an impression of one of the vocabulary words from Act II, while the other person tries to guess which word it is. After identifying correctly, students need to use words in an original sentence. Continue play until all vocabulary from Act II has been covered. Students may use their prereading vocabulary sheets as a resource for this activity.

NOTE: Explain to students that you will be having writing conferences in the next class session. During the writing conference, you will discuss their writing skills individually, based on their second writing assignment in this unit.

LESSON ELEVEN

Objectives
1. To evaluate students' writing
2. To preview prereading vocabulary and study guide questions for Act III pages 92-107
3. To silently read Act III pages 92-107
4. To have students revise their Writing Assignment 2 papers

Activity #1

Assign the prereading vocabulary pages, study guide questions and reading of Act III pages 92-107. Students should work on this independently while they are waiting for their conference with you.

Activity #2

Call students to your desk (or some other private area) to discuss their papers from Writing Assignment 2. Use the following Writing Evaluation Form to help structure your conference. Give students a date when their revisions are due. Give them about three days from the date they receive their papers to complete the revision. I suggest grading the revisions on an A-C-E scale (all revisions well-done, some revisions made, few or no revisions made). This will speed your grading time and still give some credit for the students' efforts.

WRITING EVALUATION FORM - *The Miracle Worker*

Name _____ Date _____

Writing Assignment #____ for *The Miracle Worker* unit   Grade _____

Circle One For Each Item:

Description (paragraph 1)	excellent	good	fair	poor
Plans (body paragraphs)	excellent	workable	fair	not realistic
Conclusion	excellent	good	fair	poor
Grammar:	excellent	good	fair	poor (errors noted)
Spelling:	excellent	good	fair	poor (errors noted)
Punctuation:	excellent	good	fair	poor (errors noted)
Legibility:	excellent	good	fair	poor

Strengths:

Weaknesses:

Comments/Suggestions:

LESSON TWELVE

Objectives
1. To read Act III pages 92-107
2. To give students practice reading orally
3. To give the teacher the opportunity to evaluate students' oral reading
4. To preview the prereading vocabulary and study guide questions from Act III pages 107-122

Activity # 1

Have students read their assigned parts for this section of reading. Continue to fill out an oral reading evaluation form for each student as they read their parts. If you do not finish during this reading session complete during Lesson 13.

Activity #2

Have students complete the upcoming (Act III pages 107-122) vocabulary worksheet and preview the study questions for these pages. Allow time for practice reading of these pages for next reading in class.

LESSON THIRTEEN

Objectives
1. To read Act III pages 107-122
2. To give students practice reading orally
3. To give the teacher the opportunity to evaluate students' oral reading

Activity

Have students read their assigned parts for this section of reading. Continue to fill out an oral reading evaluation form for each student as they read their parts.

LESSON FOURTEEN

Objective
    To review and reinforce the vocabulary and study guide questions for Act III

Activity #1
    Have students pair up and review all the vocabulary and study guide questions from Act III.

Activity #2
    Duplicate the matching section of the two vocabulary pages from Act III. Have students number for one set of seven and one set of ten and fill in what they think are the correct answers. Now, use the multiple choice study guide questions from Act III as a quiz to test students' reading of assigned text and as a review of the main ideas.(Use same paper as for above quiz) Exchange papers to check. Discuss answers to insure understanding. Encourage note taking for their later study use.

LESSON FIFTEEN

Objectives
    To give students practice in writing to express personal ideas

Activity
    Distribute Writing Assignment #3 and discuss the directions in detail. Allow the remaining class time for students to complete the assignment.

WRITING ASSIGNMENT #3 - *The Miracle Worker*

PROMPT

You have been a part of the inspirational story of Annie Sullivan persevering as "Teacher" to communicate with and enlighten Helen Keller. It is a powerful and influential tale that will no doubt stay with you for a long time. Without Annie Sullivan's patience and courage, Helen Keller's life very well may have been another story completely.

Your assignment is to share an experience when you were able to influence someone in a meaningful way by teaching them something.

PREWRITING

The first thing you need to do is to think of time you were successful in teaching some lesson to someone. It may be as simple as teaching your younger brother or sister to ride a bike or as complex as helping a friend overcome some major problem in their life. What qualities did you display that allowed you to influence the other person? Jot down your thoughts, feelings, opinions, or any other ideas you may have about the lesson you were able to offer someone.

DRAFTING

Begin your paper with an introductory paragraph giving your audience some background information about yourself and the learner in this situation. This paragraph's purpose is to lead into the body of your composition, which is coming next.

The body of your composition should contain the information generated from your thoughts and responses to the questions in the prewriting section. Write narrative, sequential paragraphs until you have covered each of the ideas generated in your prewriting adequately.

Finish your composition with a concluding paragraph in which you express your final statements and feelings about your role in teaching someone something meaningful.

PROMPT

When you finish your rough draft, ask a student who sits near you to read it. After reading your rough draft, he/she should tell you what he/she liked best about your work, which parts were difficult to understand, and ways in which your work could be improved. Reread your paper considering your critic's comments and make the corrections you think are necessary.

PROOFREADING

Do a final proofreading of your paper double-checking your grammar, spelling, organization, and the clarity of your ideas.

LESSONS SIXTEEN AND SEVENTEEN

Objectives:
1. To discuss the ideas and themes from *The Miracle Worker* in greater detail
2. To have students exercise their interpretive and critical thinking skills
3. To relate some of the ideas in *The Miracle Worker* to the students' lives
4. To give students the opportunity to share any extra activities or writing assignments they have completed

Activity #1

Choose the questions from the Extra Discussion Questions/Writing Assignments which seem most appropriate for your students. A class discussion of these questions is most effective if students have been given the opportunity to formulate answers to the questions prior to the discussion. To this end, you may either have all the students formulate answers to all the questions, divide your class into groups and assign one or more questions to each group, or you could assign one question to each student in your class. The option you choose will make a difference in the amount of class time needed for this activity.

Activity #2

After students have had ample time to formulate answers to the questions, begin your class discussion of the questions and the ideas presented by the questions. Be sure students take notes during the discussion so they have information to study for the unit test.

Activity #3

Give those students who have completed any extra activities related to this unit the opportunity to share now. If students would like to share their writing assignments, do this now.

EXTRA DISCUSSION QUESTIONS/WRITING ASSIGNMENTS
The Miracle Worker

Interpretive

1. How does the time period influence the thinking of the characters?

2. Describe the setting. How does it influence the action of the play?

3. Are any of the characters in *The Miracle Worker* stereotypes? If so, explain the usefulness of employing stereotypes in the play. If they are not, explain how they merit individuality.

4. What are the main conflicts in the play, and how are they resolved?

5. Describe the relationship between James and Captain Keller.

6. Give a complete character analysis of Annie Sullivan.

7. Describe the relationship between Katie and Annie Sullivan.

8. What function do the characters Jimmy Sullivan and Anagnos serve in the play?

9. Define foreshadowing. List any examples of this used in the play.

10. Define flashback. What purpose does the recurring flashback serve in the play?

11. Describe Gibson's portrayal of the Kellers. How does it influence our perception of the family?

Critical

12. Explain the significance of the title "*The Miracle Worker*".

13. We are aware that Annie will be successful with Helen before we even read the play. Despite this fact, how does Gibson hold our interest through the events of the play from the beginning to the climax?

14. Interpret Annie's statement, " I think God must owe me a resurrection."

15. Why did Captain Keller find it appalling that Annie was an independent young woman? Would people think it odd today? Why or why not? What does this say about his character? the time period?

16. Compare and contrast Kate and Annie.

The Miracle Worker Extra Discussion Questions page 2

17. Why was Annie so tough on Helen compared to how her family treated her?

18. Give a rationale for the three divisions made in the play.

19. Annie did or did not do the right thing by removing Helen from her familiar surroundings and family members. Defend your choice.

20. What universal themes are present in *The Miracle Worker*?

21. What else could the Kellers have done with Helen before Annie came to Ivy Green? Would Helen have been "better off" in an institution? Explain your answer.

22. How would Helen's life have been different if she had not been born into a well-to-do Southern family during this time period?

23. Why does Annie continue to hear her brother's pleas throughout the play? For what reason do you think they end during the last scene?

Critical/Personal Response

24. Would you consider this play an inspiration ? Why or why not?

25. *The Miracle Worker* is a short play covering, basically, a two week period. Could anything have been gained by including more scenes from the time before or after the events of the story? If so, what could have been added and for what purpose? If not, explain why not.

26. If you were Annie, what do you think you would have done about Helen stabbing you with a needle, knocking out your tooth with the doll, or locking you in your room?

27. Who was responsible for the breakthrough Helen ultimately had? Defend your answer.

28. Why were there allusions and references to the Civil War throughout the play?

29. Annie's brother's name and Helen's half- brother's name were the same. How did Annie interpret this coincidence? How do you?

30. Did living in the institution make Annie strong like she professed?

The Miracle Worker Extra Discussion Questions page 3

<u>Personal Response</u>

31. Suppose your brother or sister was a child such as Helen. Compare your feelings about her to those of James.

32. What does the word 'splendiloquent' mean when Annie refers to how she looks in her new glasses to the Perkins' girls?

33. What is the value of considering "giving up" to be the original sin like Annie told James?

34. Would you like to be a teacher of the blind and/ or deaf? Explain why or why not.

35. Explain the statement- 'language is more to the mind than light to the eye'.

<u>Quotations</u>

1. "She only dug Martha's eyes out. Almost dug. It's always almost, no point worrying till it happens, is there? You really ought to put her away, Father. It's the kindest thing."

2. "I've done as much as I can bear, I can't give my whole life to it! The house is at sixes and sevens from morning till night over the child, it's time some attention was paid to Mildred here instead!"

3. "Katie, some way of teaching her an iota of discipline has to be-"

4. "Every day she slips farther away. And I don't know how to call her back."

5. "I think God must owe me a resurrection."

6. "This is my last time to counsel you, Annie, and you do lack some I mean all-what, tact or talent to bend. To others. Annie, be-humble. It is not as if you have so many offers to pick and choose. You will need their affection, working with this child."

7. "So, you are no longer our pupil, we throw you in to the world, a teacher. If the child can be taught. No one expects you to work miracles, even for twenty-five dollars a month."

8. "Mrs. Keller, don't lose heart just because I'm not on my last legs. I have three big advantages over Dr. Howe that money couldn't buy for you. One is his work behind me, I've read every word he wrote about it and he wasn't exactly what you'd call a man of few words. Another is to be young, why, I've got energy to do anything. The third is, I've been blind."

9. "Language is to the mind more than light is to the eye. Dr. Howe says that."

The Miracle Worker Extra Discussion Questions page 4

10. "I couldn't think of it, Miss Sullivan. You'll find in the South we- view women as flowers of civiliza-"

11. 'This child has more sense than all these men Kellers, it there's ever any way to reach that mind of hers."

12. "Annie, when are we goin' home? You promised!"

13. "I hope this is not a sample of what we may expect from you. In the way of simplifying the work of looking after Helen."

14. "You devil. You think I'm so easily gotten rid of? You have a thing or two to learn, first. I have nothing else to do. And nowhere to go."

15. "The greatest, problem, I, have, is, how, to, discipline, her, without, breaking, her, spirit. But, I, shall, insist, on, reasonable, obedience, from, the, start-"

16. "Ho, there's nothing impaired in that head, it works like a mousetrap!"

17. "We catch our flies with honey, I'm afraid. We haven't the heart for much else, and so many times she simply cannot be compelled."

18. "The, more, I, think, the, more, certain, I, am, that, obedience, is, the, gateway, through, which, knowledge, enters, the, mind, of, the, child-"

19. 'This child never gives me a minute's worry."

20. "Annie. Does it hurt, to be dead?" You said we'd be together, forever and ever and ever-"

21. "I don't think Helen's worst handicap is deafness or blindness. I think it's your love. And pity. She has to be dependent on me. For everything. The food she eats, the clothes she wears, fresh air, yes, the air she breathes, whatever her body needs is a -primer, to teach her out of.

22. "No, it made me strong. But I don't think you need send Helen there. She's strong enough."

23. "You won't open her. Why can't you let her be? Have some-pity on her, for being what she is-

24. "I can't understand it, I had every intention of dismissing that girl, not setting her up like an empress."

25. "That's not the question. Stand up to the world, Jimmie, that comes first."

The Miracle Worker Extra Discussion Questions page 5

26. "Spell it! If she ever learns, you'll have a lot to tell each other, start now,"

27. "Miss Sullivan, I think you ask too much of her and yourself. God may not have meant for Helen to have the - eyes you speak of."

28. "But that battle is dead and done with, why not let it stay buried?"

29. "I don't know how. I know without it- to do nothing but obey is - no gift, obedience without understanding is a -blindness, too. Is that all I've wished on her?

30. To let her have her way in everything is a lie, to her. You've got to stand between that lie and her."

31. "She's right, Kate's right, I'm right, and you're wrong. If you drive her away from here it will be over my dead-chair, has it never occurred to you that on one occasion you might be consummately wrong?"

32. "I, love, Helen. Forever, and-ever."

LESSON EIGHTEEN

Objectives
To review all of the vocabulary work done in this unit

Activity
Choose one (or more) of the vocabulary review activities listed on the next page(s) and spend your class period as directed in the activity. Some of the materials for these review activities are located in the vocabulary resource section in this unit.

VOCABULARY REVIEW ACTIVITIES

1. Divide your class into two teams and have an old-fashioned spelling or definition bee.
2. Give each of your students (or students in groups of two, three or four) a *The Miracle Worker* Vocabulary Word Search Puzzle. The person (group) to find all of the vocabulary words in the puzzle first wins.
3. Give students a *The Miracle Worker* Vocabulary Word Search Puzzle without the word list. The person or group to find the most vocabulary words in the puzzle wins.
4. Use a *The Miracle Worker* Vocabulary Crossword Puzzle. Put the puzzle onto a transparency on the overhead projector (so everyone can see it), and do the puzzle together as a class.
5. Give students a *The Miracle Worker* Vocabulary Matching Worksheet to do.
6. Divide your class into two teams. Use *The Miracle Worker* vocabulary words with their letters jumbled as a word list. Student 1 from Team A faces off against Student 1 from Team B. You write the first jumbled word on the board. The first student (1A or 1B) to unscramble the word wins the chance for his/her team to score points. If 1A wins the jumble, go to student 2A and give him/her a definition. He/she must give you the correct spelling of the vocabulary word which fits that definition. If he/she does, Team A scores a point, and you give student 3A a definition for which you expect a correctly spelled matching vocabulary word. Continue giving Team A definitions until some team member makes an incorrect response. An incorrect response sends the game back to the jumbled-word face off, this time with students 2A and 2B. Instead of repeating giving definitions to the first few students of each team, continue with the student after the one who gave the last incorrect response on the team. For example, if Team B wins the jumbled-word face-off, and student 5B gave the last incorrect answer for Team B, you would start this round of definition questions with student 6B, and so on. The team with the most points wins!
7. Have students write a story in which they correctly use as many vocabulary words as possible. Have students read their compositions orally! Post the most original compositions on your bulletin board!

LESSON NINETEEN

Objective
To review the main ideas presented in *The Miracle Worker*

Activity #1
Choose one of the review games/activities included in the packet and spend your class period as outlined there. Some materials for these activities are located in the unit resources section of this unit.

Activity #2
Remind students that the Unit Test will be in the next class meeting. Stress the review of the Study Guides and their class notes as a last minute, brush-up review for homework.

Optional Project
Seeing and Hearing Through Your Hands

Part A
1. Provide time for students to locate resources that explain and illustrate both Braille and Sign Language.
2. Challenge them to learn the alphabet in both styles of communication. Also have them practice and learn simple terms like "yes " and "no" in sign language.
3. When you feel that your students have a basic mastery of these concepts, move on to the next culminating activity.

Part B.
1. Give each student a tagboard strip.
2. Have them represent their first names in Braille by using glue sprinkled lightly with sand. Students need to label the back of their tagboard strips with their written names. Allow time to dry.
3. Place students in small groups of five or six or smaller depending on class size.
4. Retrieve their tagboard strips from them by group and have them blindfold each other.
5. Shuffle name cards by group and hand out randomly to same group, being sure not to give own name to any student.
6. Each group will then feel the Braille on the name card and try to locate the individual to which the card belongs within their group, one by one. This could happen simultaneously, or each group could come forward in front of the class and perform in front of the rest of the class. If it is done this way, you would only hand out cards and blindfold right before each group began.

7. When a group member has deciphered the code and located the individual, they must then convert to the use of sign language to ask the individual "Are you _____? " If it is a correct match the card owner must sign back to the inquirer, "yes". If it is an incorrect match, the decoder must try once again to locate the card owner until they are correct. When a correct match is made and signed, the decoder removes his/her blindfold and enjoys watching the next decoder try to make a match.

REVIEW GAMES/ACTIVITIES - *The Miracle Worker*

1. Ask the class to make up a unit test for *The Miracle Worker*. The test should have 4 sections: matching, true/false, short answer, and essay. Students may use 1/2 period to make the test and then swap papers and use the other 1/2 class period to take a test a classmate has devised. (open book) You may want to use the unit test included in this packet or take questions from the students' unit tests to formulate your own test.

2. Take 1/2 period for students to make up true and false questions (including the answers). Collect the papers and divide the class into two teams. Draw a big tic-tac-toe board on the chalk board. Make one team X and one team O. Ask questions to each side, giving each student one turn. If the question is answered correctly, that students' team's letter (X or O) is placed in the box. If the answer is incorrect, no mark is placed in the box. The object is to get three marks in a row like tic-tac-toe. You may want to keep track of the number of games won for each team.

3. Take 1/2 period for students to make up questions (true/false and short answer). Collect the questions. Divide the class into two teams. You'll alternate asking questions to individual members of teams A & B (like in a spelling bee). The question keeps going from A to B until it is correctly answered, then a new question is asked. A correct answer does not allow the team to get another question. Correct answers are +2 points; incorrect answers are -1 point.

4. Give students a *The Miracle Worker* crossword puzzle to complete.

5. Divide your class into two teams. Use *The Miracle Worker* crossword words with their letters jumbled as a word list. Student 1 from Team A faces off against Student 1 from Team B. You write the first jumbled word on the board. The first student (1A or 1B) to unscramble the word wins the chance for his/her team to score points. If 1A wins the jumble, go to student 2A and give him/her a clue. He/she must give you the correct word which matches that clue. If he/she does, Team A scores a point, and you give student 3A a clue for which you expect another correct response. Continue giving Team A clues until some team member makes an incorrect response. An incorrect response sends the game back to the jumbled-word face off, this time with students 2A and 2B. Instead of repeating giving clues to the first few students of each team, continue with the student after the one who gave the last incorrect response on the team. For example, if Team B wins the jumbled-word face-off, and student 5B gave the last incorrect answer for Team B, you would start this round of clue questions with student 6B, and so on.

UNIT TESTS

SHORT ANSWER UNIT TEST #1 - *The Miracle Worker*

I. Matching

____ 1. MOVABLE EYELIDS   A. Torn off Aunt Ev's dress for doll's eyes by Helen

____ 2. NEEDLE   B. Playthings for Annie and Jimmy in asylum

____ 3. OBEDIENCE   C. Blind school in Boston

____ 4. CROCHET   D. Helens makes a string of wool by doing this

____ 5. THREE   E. Helen's younger sibling

____ 6. MILDRED   F. Used to jab Annie

____ 7. PERKINS INSTITUTE   G. Town in Alabama where Kellers reside

____ 8. PAPER DOLLS   H. Promise of love to Jimmy and then Helen

____ 9. FOREVER AND EVER   I. Martha and Percy play with these

____ 10. CAPTAIN KELLER   J. Doll blind girls give Annie for Helen has these

____ 11. TUSCUMBIA   K. Number of acts in play

____ 12. RATS   L. Views women as the flowers of civilization

____ 13. 25   M. Gateway through which knowledge enters mind

____ 14. BUTTONS   N. Annie's mentor from Perkins Institute

____ 15. ANAGNOS   O. Number of dollars a week Annie is paid

The Miracle Worker Short Answer Unit Test 1 Page 2

II. Short Answer

1. How does the family compensate for Helen's affliction?

2. What three advantages does Annie tell Kate she has over another governess?

3. Tell Annie's response to Kate's question, "What will you try to teach her first?"

4. Describe Annie's reaction to Helen spitting the hidden key out of her mouth and hiding it in the well.

5. What does Annie feel is her greatest obstacle with Helen?

6. What does Annie think is Helen's worst handicap?

7. For what does Annie request from the Kellers if she is to stay on there with them?

8. In what way does Annie respond to James' warning that she ought to just accept Helen's condition?

The Miracle Worker Short Answer Unit Test 1 Page 3

9. Of what use is Percy to Annie the first night alone with Helen?

10. How does Annie think Helen can come out of her shell, like the chick?

11. Does Annie agree with Captain Keller's compliment that Helen's cleanliness is next to Godliness?

12. How does Annie feel upon Helen's return to the main house?

13. Annie defines obedience without understanding as what?

14. Where does Annie take Helen when she removes her from the table? What happens there?

15. What does Annie sign and whisper to Helen that shows she can now move ahead in her own life?

The Miracle Worker Short Answer Unit Test 1 page 4

III. Essay

    Annie did or did not do the right thing by removing Helen from her familiar surroundings and family members? Defend your choice.

The Miracle Worker Short Answer Unit Test 1 page 5

IV. Vocabulary

   Listen to the vocabulary words and spell them. After you have spelled all the words, go back and write down the definitions.

1.

2.

3.

4.

5.

6.

7.

8.

9.

10.

KEY: SHORT ANSWER UNIT TEST #1 - *The Miracle Worker*

I. Matching/Identify

J - 1. MOVABLE EYELIDS   A. Torn off Aunt Ev's dress for doll's eyes by Helen

F - 2. NEEDLE   B. Playthings for Annie and Jimmy in asylum

M - 3. OBEDIENCE   C. Blind school in Boston

D - 4. CROCHET   D. Helens makes a string of wool by doing this

K - 5. THREE   E. Helen's younger sibling

E - 6. MILDRED   F. Used to jab Annie

C - 7. PERKINS INSTITUTE   G. Town in Alabama where Kellers reside

I - 8. PAPER DOLLS   H. Promise of love to Jimmy and then Helen

H - 9. FOREVER AND EVER   I. Martha and Percy play with these

L - 10. CAPTAIN KELLER   J. Doll blind girls give Annie for Helen has these

G - 11. TUSCUMBIA   K. Number of acts in play

B - 12. RATS   L. Views women as the flowers of civilization

O - 13. 25   M. Gateway through which knowledge enters mind

A - 14. BUTTONS   N. Annie's mentor from Perkins Institute

N - 15. ANAGNOS   O. Number of dollars a week Annie is paid

II. Short Answer

1. How does the family compensate for Helen's affliction?
    They allow her to do as she pleases despite the havoc it wreaks.

2. What three advantages does Annie tell Kate she has over another governess?
    When Kate is dismayed at Annie's youth, she tells Kate that she has Dr. Howe's work behind her, she is young and energetic, and that she has been blind.

3. Tell Annie's response to Kate's question, "What will you try to teach her first?"
   She tells Kate that it will be language, for language is to the mind more than light is to the eye.

4. Describe Annie's reaction to Helen spitting the hidden key out of her mouth and hiding it in the well.
   Annie is amused and challenged by Helen's apparent intelligence and guile.

5. What does Annie feel is her greatest obstacle with Helen?
   She feels her greatest problem is how to discipline her without breaking her spirit.

6. What does Annie think is Helen's worst handicap?
   She feels the family's love and pity is Helen's worst handicap.

7. For what does Annie request from the Kellers if she is to stay on there with them?
   She informs them that Helen needs to be dependent upon her for everything in order for her to teach her. She wants to be isolated with Helen for awhile.

8. In what way does Annie respond to James' warning that she ought to just accept Helen's condition?
   Her idea of giving up is that it was the original sin.

9. Of what use is Percy to Annie the first night alone with Helen?
   Since Annie will not touch Annie, she uses Percy as a familiar person to bridge the gap. Annie spells milk into Percy's hand, pushing Helen's curious hand away. Helen then wants Annie to spell only to her.

10. How does Annie think Helen can come out of her shell, like the chick?
    By learning that her fingers can talk.

11. Does Annie agree with Captain Keller's compliment that Helen's cleanliness is next to Godliness?
    No, she says it is next to nothing, Helen must learn that everything has a name.

12. How does Annie feel upon Helen's return to the main house?
    She feels like a defeated general on a deserted battlefield.

13. Annie defines obedience without understanding as what?
    She says obedience without understanding is a blindness, too.

14. Where does Annie take Helen when she removes her from the table? What happens there?
    Annie wants Helens to refill the pitcher at the pump. This is where the miracle happens. Helen comprehends that the water she feels and the fingering Annie is doing are the same thing. She utters the sounds she could speak at six months, wah-wah.

15. What does Annie sign and whisper to Helen that shows she can now move ahead in her own life?
    Annie signs and whispers I, love, Helen, forever, and ever. She no longer hears the voices from her past.

III. Essay
    Annie did or did not do the right thing by removing Helen from her familiar surroundings and family members? Defend your choice. Answers will vary.

IV. Vocabulary
    Choose ten of the vocabulary words to read orally for the vocabulary section of this unit test.

SHORT ANSWER UNIT TEST 2 *The Miracle Worker*

I. Matching/Identify

____ 1. SMOKED GLASSES   A. Playwright

____ 2. BOSTON   B. Driven to pick up Annie at the train station

____ 3. JIMMY SULLIVAN   C. Gateway through which knowledge enters mind

____ 4. CARRIAGE   D. Playthings for Annie and Jimmy in asylum

____ 5. RATS   E. Perkins Institute location

____ 6. GIBSON   F. Annie's mentor from Perkins Institute

____ 7. PITCHER   G. Focal point of play stage

____ 8. OBEDIENCE   H. Institution where Jimmy died

____ 9. TRAIN   I. How Annie traveled from Boston to Alabama

____ 10. JAMES   J. Haunting voice in Annie's mind

____ 11. ANAGNOS   K. Thinks half-sister Helen should be in asylum

____ 12. CROCHET   L. Annie's trademark

____ 13. TEWKSBURY   M. Home for Annie and Helen for two weeks

____ 14. PUMP   N. Helens makes a string of wool by doing this

____ 15. GARDEN HOUSE   O. Needed to be refilled at the pump

The Miracle Worker Short Answer Unit Test 2 Page 2

II. Short Answer

1. How does Kate discover her baby is blind and deaf?

2. Why is Helen troubled by Aunt Ev's towel doll? How does she remedy the situation?

3. Helen's half-brother, James, holds what opinion of her?

4. List three pieces of information we learn from Mr. Anagnos' farewell conversation with Annie Sullivan at the Perkins Institute.

5. What word does Annie sign to Helen first? Why?

6. What does Annie feel is her greatest obstacle with Helen?

7. How does Kate respond when Annie questions her for rewarding Helen for stabbing her with the needle?

The Miracle Worker Short Answer Unit Test 2 Page 3

8. For what reason does Annie insist everyone leave the dining room during breakfast?

9. Describe Annie's report to Kate after her ordeal with Helen and Kate's response.

10. When Kate shares her fear of sending Helen to an asylum, what do we learn about Annie's past?

11. What is wrong with Helen's eighteen nouns and three verbs?

12. Annie wants words to take the place of what for Helen?

13. How does Helen behave during her special 'welcome home' dinner?

14. Where does Annie take Helen when she removes her from the table? What happens there?

15. What does Annie sign and whisper to Helen that shows she can now move ahead in her own life?

The Miracle Worker Short Answer Unit Test 2 Page 4

III. Essay

Explain Annie's concern as expressed to Captain Keller. "To do nothing but obey is no gift, obedience without understanding is a blindness, too."

IV. Vocabulary

Listen to the vocabulary words and spell them. After you have spelled all the words, go back and write down the definitions.

1.

2.

3.

4.

5.

6.

7.

8.

9.

10.

KEY: SHORT ANSWER UNIT TEST 2 *The Miracle Worker*

I. Matching

L - 1. SMOKED GLASSES   A. Playwright

E - 2. BOSTON   B. Driven to pick up Annie at the train station

J - 3. JIMMY SULLIVAN   C. Gateway through which knowledge enters mind

B - 4. CARRIAGE   D. Playthings for Annie and Jimmy in asylum

D - 5. RATS   E. Perkins Institute location

A - 6. GIBSON   F. Annie's mentor from Perkins Institute

O - 7. PITCHER   G. Focal point of play stage

C - 8. OBEDIENCE   H. Institution where Jimmy died

I - 9. TRAIN   I. How Annie traveled from Boston to Alabama

K - 10. JAMES   J. Haunting voice in Annie's mind

F - 11. ANAGNOS   K. Thinks half-sister Helen should be in asylum

N - 12. CROCHET   L. Annie's trademark

H - 13. TEWKSBURY   M. Home for Annie and Helen for two weeks

G - 14. PUMP   N. Helens makes a string of wool by doing this

M - 15. GARDEN HOUSE   O. Needed to be refilled at the pump

II. Short Answer

1. How does Kate discover her baby is blind and deaf?
    When Kate passes her hand before Helen's eyes and snaps her fingers, there is no response. She then calls out directly at her ears and again there is no response from the baby.

2. Why is Helen troubled by Aunt Ev's towel doll? How does she remedy the situation?
   The dolls has no eyes. She rips two buttons from Aunt Ev's dress and insists they be sewn on for eyes.

3. Helen's half-brother, James, holds what opinion of her?
   He thinks she should be put in an asylum.

4. List three pieces of information we learn from Mr. Anagnos' farewell conversation with Annie Sullivan at the Perkins Institute.
   We learn that Annie has a painful past, that she is a strong-willed young woman, and that she has no other offers.

5. What word does Annie sign to Helen first? Why?
   She first signs the word doll to accompany the new doll the girls have sent for her.

6. What does Annie feel is her greatest obstacle with Helen?
   She feels her greatest problem is how to discipline her without breaking her spirit.

7. How does Kate respond when Annie questions her for rewarding Helen for stabbing her with the needle?
   Kate claims that they prefer to catch their flies with honey and regrets that they don't have the heart for much else.

8. For what reason does Annie insist everyone leave the dining room during breakfast?
   She insists they leave so she can try to train Helen uninterrupted by earlier habits allowed by the family.

9. Describe Annie's report to Kate after her ordeal with Helen and Kate's response.
   Worse for the wear, Annie flatly informs her that the room is a wreck, but Helen ate from her own plate and folded her napkin. Kate is beside herself with emotion.

10. When Kate shares her fear of sending Helen to an asylum, what do we learn about Annie's past?
    She shares that she grew up in such a place. She tells of the horrors and of her dead brother, Jimmy. She says it made her strong, but that Helen is strong enough already.

11. What is wrong with Helen's eighteen nouns and three verbs?
    Annie is exasperated because they are just a finger-game to her with no meaning.

12. Annie wants words to take the place of what for Helen?
    She wants words to be her eyes to everything in the world.

13. How does Helen behave during her special 'welcome home' dinner?
    She reverts back to the same behavior she used when eating with her family earlier.

14. Where does Annie take Helen when she removes her from the table? What happens there?
    Annie wants Helens to refill the pitcher at the pump. This is where the miracle happens. Helen comprehends that the water she feels and the fingering Annie is doing are the same thing. She utters the sounds she could speak at six months, wah-wah.

15. What does Annie sign and whisper to Helen that shows she can now move ahead in her own life?
    Annie signs and whispers I, love, Helen, forever, and ever. She no longer hears the voices from her past.

III. Essay
    Explain Annie's concern as expressed to Captain Keller. "To do nothing but obey is no gift, obedience without understanding is a blindness, too."   (Answers will vary.)

IV. Vocabulary
    Choose ten of the vocabulary words to read orally for the vocabulary section of the test.

ADVANCED SHORT ANSWER UNIT TEST - *The Miracle Worker*

I. Matching

____ 1. SMOKED GLASSES   A. Playwright

____ 2. BOSTON   B. Driven to pick up Annie at the train station

____ 3. JIMMY SULLIVAN   C. Gateway through which knowledge enters mind

____ 4. CARRIAGE   D. Playthings for Annie and Jimmy in asylum

____ 5. RATS   E. Perkins Institute location

____ 6. GIBSON   F. Annie's mentor from Perkins Institute

____ 7. PITCHER   G. Focal point of play stage

____ 8. OBEDIENCE   H. Institution where Jimmy died

____ 9. TRAIN   I. How Annie traveled from Boston to Alabama

____ 10. JAMES   J. Haunting voice in Annie's mind

____ 11. ANAGNOS   K. Thinks half-sister Helen should be in asylum

____ 12. CROCHET   L. Annie's trademark

____ 13. TEWKSBURY   M. Home for Annie and Helen for two weeks

____ 14. PUMP   N. Helens makes a string of wool by doing this

____ 15. GARDEN HOUSE   O. Needed to be refilled at the pump

The Miracle Worker Advanced Short Answer Unit Test Page 2

II. Short Answer

1. Describe the relationship between James and Captain Keller.

2. Explain the significance of the title "*The Miracle Worker*".

3. Why does Annie continue to hear her brother's pleas throughout the play? Why do you think they end during the last scene?

4. Why did the author include allusions and references to the Civil War throughout the play?

5. What does Annie mean by "I think God must owe me a resurrection?"

6. Explain the statement: "Language is more to the mind than light to the eye."

The Miracle Worker Advanced Short Answer Unit Test Page 3

III. Quotations: Explain the importance and meaning of the following quotations.

1. "You devil. You think I'm so easily gotten rid of? You have a thing or two to learn, first. I have nothing else to do. And nowhere to go."

2. "We catch our flies with honey, I'm afraid. We haven't the heart for much else, and so many times she simply cannot be compelled."

3. "The, more, I, think, the, more, certain, I, am, that, obedience, is, the, gateway, through, which, knowledge, enters, the, mind, of, the, child-"

4. " I don't think Helen's worst handicap is deafness or blindness. I think it's your love. And pity.

5. "No, it made me strong. But I don't think you need send Helen there. She's strong enough."

6. "I don't know how. I know without it- to do nothing but obey is - no gift, obedience without understanding is a -blindness, too. Is that all I've wished on her?

The Miracle Worker Advanced Short Answer Unit Test Page 4

IV. Vocabulary

Listen to the vocabulary words and write them down. After you have written down all the words, write a paragraph in which you use all the words. The paragraph must in some way relate to *The Miracle Worker*.

MULTIPLE CHOICE UNIT TEST 1 - *The Miracle Worker*

I. Matching

1. GARDEN HOUSE   A. Playwright

2. YOU DEVIL   B. Dropped in the well by Helen

3. GIBSON   C. Helen's mind works like one

4. WATER   D. Number of dollars a week Annie is paid

5. DOCTOR   E. Used by Annie to spell correctly

6. NAPKIN   F. Original sin according to Annie

7. MOUSETRAP   G. Diagnoses baby Helen with acute congestion

8. KEY   H. Home for Annie and Helen for two weeks

9. BOSTON   I. Playthings for Annie and Jimmy in asylum

10. GIVING UP   J. Asked for by Annie to teach Helen alone

11. NEEDLE   K. Used to jab Annie

12. 25   L. Annie called Helen this after she hid room key

13. ANOTHER WEEK   M. Perkins Institute location

14. DICTIONARY   N. Folded by Helen

15. RATS   O. Breakthrough word for Helen

The Miracle Worker Multiple Choice Unit Test 1 page 2

II. Multiple Choice

1. Helen's half-brother, James Keller, thinks
    a. Helen should be put in an asylum.
    b. Helen is an eyesore.
    c. Helen is to pitied.
    d. all of the above

2. Select the one piece of information we do *not* learn from Mr. Anagnos' farewell conversation with Annie Sullivan at the Perkins Institute.
    a. Annie has no other offers other than the Kellers.
    b. Annie is a strong-willed young woman.
    c. Annie and her brother played with rats in the almshouse.
    d. Annie has a painful past

3. Which of the following is *not* an advantage Annie tells Kate she has over another governess?
    a. She has been blind.
    b. She has lived in an asylum.
    c. She has Dr. Howe's work behind her.
    d. She is young and energetic.

4. How does Annie's respond to Kate's question, "What will you try to teach her first?"
    a. It will be language, for language is to the mind more than light is to the eye.
    b. It will be love, for all important is learned through love.
    c. It will be obedience, for nothing can be gained without discipline.
    d. It will be repetition, because it is the pathway for learning.

5. Helen first responds to Annie Sullivan by
    a. boldly feeling her arms and her face.
    b. dragging Annie's suitcase up the stairs to her prepared room.
    c. ignoring her and retreating to the pump.
    d. grabbing the doll and hugging it tightly.

6. Annie's reaction to Helen spitting the key out of her mouth and hiding it in the well is one of which
    a. she is noticeably upset and considering leaving before she unpacks.
    b. she is terrified that Helen will swallow it and choke.
    c. she is amused and challenged by Helen's apparent intelligence and guile.
    d. she has no patience for such behavior.

The Miracle Worker Multiple Choice Unit Test 1 page 3

7. Annie feels her greatest obstacle with Helen is
   a. how to get Helen to trust her.
   b. how to rid her of all of her earlier learned habits.
   c. how to discipline her without breaking her spirit.
   d. how to get Helen to behave properly at the dinner table.

8. How does Kate respond when Annie questions her for rewarding Helen for stabbing her with the needle?
   a. She claims that they prefer to catch their flies with honey.
   b. She regrets that they don't have the heart for much else.
   c. She says Helen simply cannot be compelled at times.
   d. all of the above

9. What question does Kate ask Captain Keller when he demands that she tell Annie to change her tactics with Helen or leave?
   a. Why must I tell her?
   b. Why don't you tell her?
   c. Where will you be?
   d. None of the above

10. When Annie finally gets Helen to take a spoonful of food from her plate into her mouth
    a. Helen spits it out at Annie
    b. Annie dashes the water from the pitcher into Helen's face.
    c. Helen smiles from pride at her accomplishment.
    d. Both a and b

11. Whose voice *doesn't* Annie hear in her mind after reviewing the Perkin's report?
    a. her brother's
    b. the old crones'
    c. the doctor's from the asylum
    d. Anagnos'

12. Annie thinks Helen's worst handicap is
    a. her lack of mental abilities.
    b. her stubbornness and curiosity.
    c. her family's love and pity .
    d. her age and gender.

The Miracle Worker Multiple Choice Unit Test 1 page 4

13. Annie tells James that her idea of the original sin is
    a. the way he snoops around all the time.
    b. giving up.
    c. Adam tempting Eve in the garden of Eden.
    d. sending a disabled child to an asylum.

14. What is 'a little tornado incarnate'?
    a. The inclement weather approaching the Alabama plains.
    b. Helen's reaction to her new surroundings.
    c. Annie's reaction to the Captain's criticism of her tactics with Helen.
    d. Helen's half-brother, James,' reaction to Captain Keller's agreement with Annie.

15. Annie uses what two things to get through to Helen the first night?
    a. cake and Helen's jealousy
    b. Helen's curiosity and Percy
    c. milk and cookies
    d. cake and Helen's curiosity

16. Annie thinks Helen can come out of her shell, like the chick by
    a. trying to understand that she is an intelligent little girl.
    b. learning that her new manners will impress her family.
    c. showing some affection to her teacher.
    d. learning that her fingers can talk.

17. Kate advises James to
    a. fall in love, get married, and have children to understand parenthood.
    b. stay out of her way when it comes to Helen and to treat Annie much better
    c. stand up to the world, including his father.
    d. learn to be his father's friend, as well as son.

18. Complete Annie's definition for obedience without understanding.
    a. helplessness
    b. blindness
    c. emptiness
    d. carelessness

The Miracle Worker Multiple Choice Unit Test 1 page 5

19. After the breakthrough, Helen offers to Annie
    a. the doll she gave her and signs the word doll.
    b. the water pitcher she came to fill at the pump.
    c. the keys she asked her mother for to Annie.
    d. all of her newly crocheted strings from their two weeks alone.

20. Annie can now move ahead in her own life because she
    a. has learned to love again after her brother's death.
    b. has accomplished what she set out to do with Helen.
    c. has impressed a Civil War Captain and his wife.
    d. has taught Helen that words have meaning.

The Miracle Worker Multiple Choice Unit Test 1 page 6

III. Quotations: Identify the speaker:

    A= Captain Keller   **B**= Kate   **C**= James   **D**= Aunt Ev
    E= Annie   **F**= Anagnos   **G**= Jimmy Sullivan

1. "I've done as much as I can bear, I can't give my whole life to it! The house is at sixes and sevens from morning till night over the child, it's time some attention was paid to Mildred here instead!"

2. "I think God must owe me a resurrection."

3. "So, you are no longer our pupil, we throw you in to the world, a teacher. If the child can be taught. No one expects you to work miracles, even for twenty-five dollars a month."

4. "Language is to the mind more than light is to the eye. Dr. Howe says that."

5. 'This child has more sense than all these men Kellers, it there's ever any way to reach that mind of hers."

6. "Annie, when are we goin' home? You promised!"

7. "Ho, there's nothing impaired in that head, it works like a mousetrap!"

8. "I should like to learn those letters, Miss Annie."

9. "We catch our flies with honey, I'm afraid. We haven't the heart for much else, and so many times she simply cannot be compelled."

10. "Annie. Does it hurt, to be dead?" You said we'd be together, forever and ever and ever-"

11. "You won't open her. Why can't you let her be? Have some-pity on her, for being what she is-

12. "Miss Sullivan, I think you ask too much of her and yourself. God may not have meant for Helen to have the - eyes you speak of."

13. "But that battle is dead and done with, why not let it stay buried?"

14. "She's right, Kate's right, I'm right, and you're wrong. If you drive her away from here it will be over my dead-chair, has it never occurred to you that on one occasion you might be consummately wrong?"

15. "I, love, Helen. Forever, and-ever."

The Miracle Worker Multiple Choice Unit Test 1 page 7

IV. Vocabulary (Matching)

1. REPROACHFULLY   A. Sorrowfully; sadly

2. DEPRIVATION   B. Motionless; frozen

3. AFFLICTION   C. Allusions; hints

4. CONSUMMATELY   D. Bothered; peeved

5. INDIGNANTLY   E. Righteously angry

6. PUMMELS   F. Unending; ceaseless

7. IMPERIOUS   G. Satisfying; gratifying

8. TRANSFIXED   H. Disapprovingly; critically

9. OCULIST   I. Drearily

10. INTIMATIONS   J. Evaluation

11. DEFERENTIAL   K. Respectful; obedient

12. NETTLED   L. Absolutely; perfectly

13. INTERMINABLE   M. Eye doctor

14. AVERSION   N. Lively; spirited

15. DEVOUTNESS   O. Loss

16. PLAINTIVELY   P. Thrashes; beats

17. PLACATING   Q. Distaste; dislike

18. VIVACIOUS   R. Hardship; problem

19. DOURLY   S. Godliness, piety

20. APPRAISAL   T. Urgent; pressing

MULTIPLE CHOICE UNIT TEST 2 - *The Miracle Worker*

I. Matching

1. JAMES — A. Thinks half-sister Helen should be in asylum

2. 25 — B. Asked for by Annie to teach Helen alone

3. IVY GREEN — C. Torn off Aunt Ev's dress for doll's eyes by Helen

4. PAPA — D. Number of dollars a week Annie is paid

5. ANOTHER WEEK — E. Promise of love to Jimmy and then Helen

6. GARNET RING — F. Going away present from Anagnos

7. MOVABLE EYELIDS — G. Knocked out when Helen hits Annie with doll

8. KEY — H. How Annie traveled from Boston to Alabama

9. BUTTONS — I. Dropped in the well by Helen

10. DEADHOUSE — J. Keller estate in Alabama

11. FOREVER AND EVER — K. Sign for Captain Keller

12. ANGEL — L. Blind school in Boston

13. PERKINS INSTITUTE — M. Doll blind girls give Annie for Helen has these

14. TOOTH — N. Baby Martha

15. TRAIN — O. Asylum playroom for Annie and Jimmy

The Miracle Worker Multiple Choice Unit Test 2 page 2

II. Multiple Choice

1. Kate discovers her baby is blind and deaf when
    a. the doctor announces the diagnosis.
    b. she passes her hand before the baby's eyes and there is no movement.
    c. she shouts directly at her and the baby does not react.
    d. both b and c

2. Which family member seems to be the closest to Helen?
    a. Kate
    b. James
    c. Captain Keller
    d. all of the above

3. Helen's half-brother, James Keller, thinks
    a. Helen should be put in an asylum.
    b. Helen is an eyesore.
    c. Helen is to pitied.
    d. all of the above

4. Select the one piece of information we do *not* learn from Mr. Anagnos' farewell conversation with Annie Sullivan at the Perkins Institute.
    a. Annie has no other offers other than the Kellers.
    b. Annie is a strong-willed young woman.
    c. Annie and her brother played with rats in the almshouse.
    d. Annie has a painful past.

5. Which of the following is *not* an advantage Annie tells Kate she has over another governess?
    a. She has been blind.
    b. She has lived in an asylum.
    c. She has Dr. Howe's work behind her.
    d. She is young and energetic.

6. How does Annie's respond to Kate's question , "What will you try to teach her first?"
    a. It will be language, for language is to the mind more than light is to the eye.
    b. It will be love, for all important is learned through love.
    c. It will be obedience, for nothing can be gained without discipline.
    d. It will be repetition, because it is the pathway for learning.

The Miracle Worker Multiple Choice Unit Test 2 page 3

7. Captain Keller becomes upset before dinner the day of Annie's arrival because
    a. Annie is locked in her room by Helen who has taken off with the only key.
    b. Annie has spoken offensively to him from the minute she stepped out of the carriage.
    c. Annie is not what he expected in a governess.
    d. he is hungry and tired of waiting for dinner.

8. Annie's reaction to Helen spitting the key out of her mouth and hiding it in the well is one of which
    a. she is noticeably upset and considering leaving before she unpacks.
    b. she is terrified that Helen will swallow it and choke.
    c. she is amused and challenged by Helen's apparent intelligence and guile.
    d. she has no patience for such behavior.

9. Annie feels her greatest obstacle with Helen is
    a. how to get Helen to trust her.
    b. how to rid her of all of her earlier learned habits.
    c. how to discipline her without breaking her spirit.
    d. how to get Helen to behave properly at the dinner table.

10. What question does Kate ask Captain Keller when he demands that she tell Annie to change her tactics with Helen or leave?
    a. Why must I tell her?
    b. Why don't you tell her?
    c. Where will you be?
    d. None of the above

11. When Annie finally gets Helen to take a spoonful of food from her plate into her mouth
    a. Helen spits it out at Annie
    b. Annie dashes the water from the pitcher into Helen's face.
    c. Helen smiles from pride at her accomplishment.
    d. Both a and b

12. Whose voice *doesn't* Annie hear in her mind after reviewing the Perkin's report?
    a. her brother's
    b. the old crones'
    c. the doctor's from the asylum
    d. Anagnos'

The Miracle Worker Short Answer Unit Test 2 Page 4

13. Annie thinks Helen's worst handicap is
    a. her lack of mental abilities.
    b. her stubbornness and curiosity.
    c. her family's love and pity .
    d. her age and gender.

14. Annie requests the Kellers to
    a. take Helen away to Italy where she can learn braille and sign language.
    b. allow Helen to become dependent upon her for everything.
    c. give her two weeks with Helen alone in the garden house.
    d. both b and c

15. Annie tells James that her idea of the original sin is
    a. the way he snoops around all the time.
    b. giving up.
    c. Adam tempting Eve in the garden of Eden.
    d. sending a disabled child to an asylum.

16. What is 'a little tornado incarnate'?
    a. The inclement weather approaching the Alabama plains.
    b. Helen's reaction to her new surroundings.
    c. Annie's reaction to the Captain's criticism of her tactics with Helen.
    d. Helen's half-brother, James,' reaction to Captain Keller's agreement with Annie.

17. Annie thinks Helen can come out of her shell, like the chick by
    a. trying to understand that she is an intelligent little girl.
    b. learning that her new manners will impress her family.
    c. showing some affection to her teacher.
    d. learning that her fingers can talk.

18. Helen's eighteen nouns and three verbs
    a. are just a finger-game to her with no meaning.
    b. come to her very easily.
    c. were learned in three days and five hours.
    d. can be used in a sentence by Helen.

The Miracle Worker Short Answer Unit Test 2 Page 5

19. Complete the analogy. Wings are to birds as words are to
    a. meaning
    b. humans
    c. vocal chords
    d. babies

20. Complete Annie's definition for obedience without understanding.
    a. helplessness
    b. blindness
    c. emptiness
    d. carelessness

The Miracle Worker Short Answer Unit Test 2 Page 6

III. Quotations: Identify the speaker:

A= James **B**= Captain Keller **C**= Anagnos **D**= Aunt Ev
E= Jimmy Sullivan **F**= Annie **G**=Kate

1. "I've done as much as I can bear, I can't give my whole life to it! The house is at sixes and sevens from morning till night over the child, it's time some attention was paid to Mildred here instead!"

2. "I think God must owe me a resurrection."

3. "So, you are no longer our pupil, we throw you in to the world, a teacher. If the child can be taught. No one expects you to work miracles, even for twenty-five dollars a month."

4. "Language is to the mind more than light is to the eye. Dr. Howe says that."

5. 'This child has more sense than all these men Kellers, it there's ever any way to reach that mind of hers."

6. "Annie, when are we goin' home? You promised!"

7. "Ho, there's nothing impaired in that head, it works like a mousetrap!"

8. "I should like to learn those letters, Miss Annie."

9. "We catch our flies with honey, I'm afraid. We haven't the heart for much else, and so many times she simply cannot be compelled."

10. "Annie. Does it hurt, to be dead?" You said we'd be together, forever and ever and ever-"

11. "You won't open her. Why can't you let her be? Have some-pity on her, for being what she is-"

12. "Miss Sullivan, I think you ask too much of her and yourself. God may not have meant for Helen to have the - eyes you speak of."

13. "But that battle is dead and done with, why not let it stay buried?"

14. "She's right, Kate's right, I'm right, and you're wrong. If you drive her away from here it will be over my dead-chair, has it never occurred to you that on one occasion you might be consummately wrong?"

15. "I, love, Helen. Forever, and-ever."

The Miracle Worker Multiple Choice Unit Test 2 page 7

IV. Vocabulary (Matching)

1. INDULGENT
2. RECOMMENCED
3. FORLORN
4. RESOLUTELY
5. VOLUMINOUS
6. VIGIL
7. BENIGN
8. HAGGARD
9. VEXEDLY
10. INTIMATIONS
11. APPRAISAL
12. UNAVAILING
13. IMPERIOUS
14. DIMINUTIVE
15. IMPASSIVELY
16. COMPELLED
17. COMPUNCTION
18. NETTLED
19. RELINQUISHES
20. INEXORABLY

A. Favorable; pleasant
B. Bulky; large
C. Forsaken; abandoned
D. Irritatedly
E. Relentlessly; unyielding
F. Obliged; made responsible
G. Small
H. Resigns; gives up
I. Allusions; hints
J. Urgent; pressing
K. Bothered; peeved
L. Repeated; began again
M. Permissive; lenient
N. Unemotionally
O. Care worn; drawn
P. A watch
Q. Hopeless; futile
R. Deliberately; willfully
S. Shame; regret
T. Evaluation

ANSWER SHEET - *The Miracle Worker*
Multiple Choice Unit Tests

I. Matching
1. ____
2. ____
3. ____
4. ____
5. ____
6. ____
7. ____
8. ____
9. ____
10. ____
11. ____
12. ____
13. ____
14. ____
15. ____

II. Quotes
1. (A) (B) (C) (D) (E) (F) (G) (H)
2. (A) (B) (C) (D) (E) (F) (G) (H)
3. (A) (B) (C) (D) (E) (F) (G) (H)
4. (A) (B) (C) (D) (E) (F) (G) (H)
5. (A) (B) (C) (D) (E) (F) (G) (H)
6. (A) (B) (C) (D) (E) (F) (G) (H)
7. (A) (B) (C) (D) (E) (F) (G) (H)
8. (A) (B) (C) (D) (E) (F) (G) (H)
9. (A) (B) (C) (D) (E) (F) (G) (H)
10. (A) (B) (C) (D) (E) (F) (G) (H)
11. (A) (B) (C) (D) (E) (F) (G) (H)
12. (A) (B) (C) (D) (E) (F) (G) (H)
13. (A) (B) (C) (D) (E) (F) (G) (H)
14. (A) (B) (C) (D) (E) (F) (G) (H)
15. (A) (B) (C) (D) (E) (F) (G) (H)

II. Multiple Choice
1. (A) (B) (C) (D)
2. (A) (B) (C) (D)
3. (A) (B) (C) (D)
4. (A) (B) (C) (D)
5. (A) (B) (C) (D)
6. (A) (B) (C) (D)
7. (A) (B) (C) (D)
8. (A) (B) (C) (D)
9. (A) (B) (C) (D)
10. (A) (B) (C) (D)
11. (A) (B) (C) (D)
12. (A) (B) (C) (D)
13. (A) (B) (C) (D)
14. (A) (B) (C) (D)
15. (A) (B) (C) (D)
16. (A) (B) (C) (D)
17. (A) (B) (C) (D)
18. (A) (B) (C) (D)
19. (A) (B) (C) (D)
20. (A) (B) (C) (D)

V. Vocabulary
1. ____
2. ____
3. ____
4. ____
5. ____
6. ____
7. ____
8. ____
9. ____
10. ____
11. ____
12. ____
13. ____
14. ____
15. ____
16. ____
17. ____
18. ____
19. ____
20. ____

ANSWER SHEET KEY - *The Miracle Worker*
Multiple Choice Unit Test 1

I. Matching
1. H
2. L
3. A
4. O
5. G
6. N
7. C
8. B
9. M
10. F
11. K
12. D
13. J
14. E
15. I

II. Quotes
1. ( ) (B) (C) (D) (E) (F) (G) (H)
2. (A) (B) (C) (D) ( ) (F) (G) (H)
3. (A) (B) (C) (D) (E) ( ) (G) (H)
4. (A) (B) (C) (D) ( ) (F) (G) (H)
5. (A) (B) (C) ( ) (E) (F) (G) (H)
6. (A) (B) (C) (D) (E) (F) ( ) (H)
7. (A) (B) (C) (D) ( ) (F) (G) (H)
8. (A) ( ) (C) (D) (E) (F) (G) (H)
9. (A) ( ) (C) (D) (E) (F) (G) (H)
10. (A) (B) (C) (D) (E) (F) ( ) (H)
11. (A) (B) ( ) (D) (E) (F) (G) (H)
12. ( ) (B) (C) (D) (E) (F) (G) (H)
13. (A) (B) (C) (D) (E) ( ) (G) (H)
14. (A) (B) ( ) (D) (E) (F) (G) (H)
15. (A) (B) (C) (D) ( ) (F) (G) (H)

II. Multiple Choice
1. (A) (B) (C) ( )
2. (A) (B) ( ) (D)
3. (A) ( ) (C) (D)
4. ( ) (B) (C) (D)
5. ( ) (B) (C) (D)
6. (A) (B) ( ) (D)
7. (A) (B) ( ) (D)
8. (A) (B) (C) ( )
9. (A) (B) ( ) (D)
10. (A) (B) (C) ( )
11. (A) (B) (C) ( )
12. (A) (B) ( ) (D)
13. (A) ( ) (C) (D)
14. (A) ( ) (C) (D)
15. (A) ( ) (C) (D)
16. (A) (B) (C) ( )
17. (A) (B) ( ) (D)
18. (A) ( ) (C) (D)
19. (A) (B) ( ) (D)
20. ( ) (B) (C) (D)

V. Vocabulary
1. H
2. O
3. R
4. L
5. E
6. P
7. T
8. B
9. M
10. C
11. K
12. D
13. F
14. Q
15. S
16. A
17. G
18. N
19. I
20. J

ANSWER SHEET KEY - *The Miracle Worker*
Multiple Choice Unit Test 2

I. Matching
1. A
2. D
3. J
4. K
5. B
6. F
7. M
8. I
9. C
10. O
11. E
12. N
13. L
14. G
15. H

II. Quotes
1. (A) ( ) (C) (D) (E) (F) (G) (H)
2. (A) (B) (C) (D) (E) ( ) (G) (H)
3. (A) (B) ( ) (D) (E) (F) (G) (H)
4. (A) (B) (C) (D) (E) ( ) (G) (H)
5. (A) (B) (C) ( ) (E) (F) (G) (H)
6. (A) (B) (C) (D) ( ) (F) (G) (H)
7. (A) (B) (C) (D) (E) ( ) (G) (H)
8. (A) (B) (C) (D) (E) (F) ( ) (H)
9. (A) (B) (C) (D) (E) (F) ( ) (H)
10. (A) (B) (C) (D) ( ) (F) (G) (H)
11. ( ) (B) (C) (D) (E) (F) (G) (H)
12. (A) ( ) (C) (D) (E) (F) (G) (H)
13. (A) (B) ( ) (D) (E) (F) (G) (H)
14. ( ) (B) (C) (D) (E) (F) (G) (H)
15. (A) (B) (C) (D) (E) ( ) (G) (H)

II. Multiple Choice
1. (A) (B) (C) ( )
2. ( ) (B) (C) (D)
3. (A) (B) (C) ( )
4. (A) (B) ( ) (D)
5. (A) ( ) (C) (D)
6. ( ) (B) (C) (D)
7. ( ) (B) (C) (D)
8. (A) (B) ( ) (D)
9. (A) (B) ( ) (D)
10. (A) (B) ( ) (D)
11. (A) (B) (C) ( )
12. (A) (B) (C) ( )
13. (A) (B) ( ) (D)
14. (A) (B) (C) ( )
15. (A) ( ) (C) (D)
16. (A) ( ) (C) (D)
17. (A) (B) (C) ( )
18. ( ) (B) (C) (D)
19. (A) ( ) (C) (D)
20. (A) ( ) (C) (D)

V. Vocabulary
1. M
2. L
3. C
4. R
5. B
6. P
7. A
8. O
9. D
10. I
11. T
12. Q
13. J
14. G
15. N
16. F
17. S
18. K
19. H
20. E

UNIT RESOURCE MATERIALS

BULLETIN BOARD IDEAS - *The Miracle Worker*

1. Post a large United States' map on the wall. Have students chart Annie's train trip from Boston, Massachusetts to Tuscumbia, Alabama.

2. Outline and illustrate the three main sets for the play like a mural: the Keller homestead, the garden house, and the pump area.

3. Draw one of the word search puzzles onto the bulletinboard. (Be sure to enlarge it.) Write the key words to one side. Invite students to take their pens or markers and find the words before and/or after class (or perhaps this could be an activity for students who finish their work early).

4. Reproduce the entire Braille alphabet and post in the proper sequence. Print each symbol on a separate 8 1/2 x 11" piece of index paper. Make the dots raised by applying glue on them and letting them dry. Perhaps sprinkle sand over the glue for even more distinction.

5. Display the entire sign language alphabet and other commonly used simple terms.

6. Make illustrated posters that display the words to the song Annie sang on the first night in the garden house: Mama's Gonna Buy You a Mockingbird.

7. Cut out and display large construction paper symbols that depict major ideas from the play such as: a ladder, a key, a water pump, a baby doll, dark glasses, etc.

EXTRA ACTIVITIES

One of the difficulties in teaching a novel is that all students don't read at the same speed. One student who likes to read may take the book home and finish it in a day or two. Sometimes a few students finish the in-class assignments early. The problem, then, is finding suitable extra activities for students.

One thing you can do is to keep a little library in the classroom. For this unit on *The Miracle Worker*, you might check out from the school library other play or poetry by William Gibson. A biography of the author, Helen Keller, or Annie Sullivan would be interesting for some students. You may include other related books and articles about Braille, sign language, blind and deaf education, Ivy Green Homestead, Tuscumbia, Alabama, Theatre, drama, theatrical presentations, play-writing, playwrights, the Perkins' Institute for the Blind, The Horace Mann School for the Deaf, Alexander Graham Bell in Deaf Education, Civil War, State Asylums in the 1800's, Radcliffe College, and Post Civil War sentiment in the South.

Other things you may keep on hand are puzzles. We have made some relating directly to *The Miracle Worker* for you. Feel free to duplicate them for your students.

Some students may like to draw. You might devise a contest or allow some extra-credit grade for students who draw characters or scenes from *The Miracle Worker*. Note, too, that if the students do not want to keep their drawings you may pick up some extra bulletin board materials this way. If you have a contest and you supply the prize (a CD or something like that perhaps), you could, possibly, make the drawing itself a non-refundable entry fee.

The pages which follow contain games, puzzles and worksheets. The keys, when appropriate, immediately follow the puzzle or worksheet. There are two main groups of activities: one group for the unit; that is, generally relating to The Miracle Worker text, and another group of activities related strictly to The Miracle Worker vocabulary.

Directions for the games, puzzles and worksheets are self-explanatory. The object here is to provide you with extra materials you may use in any way you choose.

MORE ACTIVITIES - *The Miracle Worker*

1. Listen to and sing the songs that are mentioned in the play: Mama's Gonna Buy You a Mockingbird, and Buffalo Girls Won't You Come Out Tonight

2. Show a film version of *The Miracle Worker* to the class after you have completed reading the play. Have students evaluate the movie and compare/contrast it with the play.

3. Have students design a book cover (front and back and inside flaps) for *The Miracle Worker*.

4. Write epitaphs for Jimmy Sullivan.

5. Invite a guest speaker to discuss deaf and blind education. Perhaps it could be a teacher form such as institute.

6. Use some of the related topics (noted earlier for an in-class library) as topics for research, reports or written papers, or as topics for guest speakers.

7. Visit a school for the Deaf and/or the Blind.

8. Attend a professional play version of *The Miracle Worker*.

9. Attend a play which has professional signers and try to watch them as closely as possible.

10. Visit Ivy Green, Tuscumbia, Alabama or view pictures of it on the Internet or in encyclopedias or tour books.

11. Write to the playwright, William Gibson, and ask him how he became interested in writing this play and from where he obtained his information.

12. Read the sequel play, *Miracle on Monday* by the same author and compare them.

13. Locate and demonstrate the use of a Braille typewriter.

14. Construct a model of Ivy Green out of clay or through a diorama.

15. Research the sentiments of the Post- Civil War South.

16. Debate the effects of spoiling a disabled child.

17. Interview any number of blind and /or deaf people. Compare their lives with yours. Share reports with the class. Chart the similarities and differences.

WORD SEARCH - Miracle Worker

```
F P I T Y E S D E A D H O U S E J K C F
O P D B L E Q Y G B O S T O N R F R R L
P B F D S F W F A B G G W G D O C T O R
P J E S R V A X U X F A X F R C C N C H
D E A D I L T W G T P R S E T R B K H S
N L P N I L E R N V W D V H W A I I E C
G K E L L E R P A R T E S U O M V K T T
R Y R E A B N H L T R N N N P Y E E T E
I F C G E D T C Z C S G I T F N A E Y Y
N W Y N K R D P E L P A I V Y C M H X L
G L N A A T S E T H R E E B H F Y C H W
J A T M F W U Y R T E B R E S R I T T N
V E J Q L E L E X K P L R K U O O V L Z
D L F I V N L L A N A C E B I O N C E R
K I V D S T I I H N P M S N T N E X S Y
R E C E C Y V D G H A K I U A G S R L J
D Z M T M S A S V I W G S L A P O Z L N
H A M L I G N R B E V C N I D S K R O N
J I M M Y O S R T N U I R O S R L I D J
K C V C L X N W D M T R N I S Q E S N L
V W T D M Q S A B C A Z C G T S C D V L
S Z L Y X V W I R C B S P I T C H E R N
Q P V D B N A M L Y W B U T T O N S W B
```

ANAGNOS	DEVIL	JAMES	OBEDIENCE	THREE
ANGEL	DICTIONARY	JIMMY	PAPA	TOOTH
ANNE	DOCTOR	KATE	PERCY	TRAIN
BELL	DOLLS	KELLER	PERKINS	TUSCUMBIA
BITE	EYELIDS	KEY	PITCHER	TWENTY
BOSTON	FOREVER	LADDER	PITY	TWENTYFIVE
BUTTONS	GARDEN	LANGUAGE	RATS	VINEY
CARRIAGE	GIBSON	MARTHA	RING	WATER
CHEEK	GIVING	MILDRED	SCISSORS	
CRAMP	GLASSES	MOUSETRAP	SULLIVAN	
CROCHET	HELEN	NAPKIN	TEACHER	
DEADHOUSE	IVY	NEEDLE	TEWKSBURY	

WORD SEARCH ANSWER KEY - Miracle Worker

ANAGNOS	DEVIL	JAMES	OBEDIENCE	THREE
ANGEL	DICTIONARY	JIMMY	PAPA	TOOTH
ANNE	DOCTOR	KATE	PERCY	TRAIN
BELL	DOLLS	KELLER	PERKINS	TUSCUMBIA
BITE	EYELIDS	KEY	PITCHER	TWENTY
BOSTON	FOREVER	LADDER	PITY	TWENTYFIVE
BUTTONS	GARDEN	LANGUAGE	RATS	VINEY
CARRIAGE	GIBSON	MARTHA	RING	WATER
CHEEK	GIVING	MILDRED	SCISSORS	
CRAMP	GLASSES	MOUSETRAP	SULLIVAN	
CROCHET	HELEN	NAPKIN	TEACHER	
DEADHOUSE	IVY	NEEDLE	TEWKSBURY	

CROSSWORD - Miracle Worker

Across
1. Used by Percy to alert family of Helen's outburst
2. Annie called Helen this after she hid the room key
5. Helen does this to her fingers in her mouth
6. Playwright
8. Annie's mentor from Perkins Institute
10. Annie has this from signing to Helen: writer's ___
11. Taken from Martha forcefully by Helen
13. Dropped by Helen into the well
15. Keller estate in Alabama: ___ Green
16. Like a little safe, locked, that no one can open
17. Helen puts her fingers in his mouth
18. Doll blind girls give Annie for Helen has movable ___

Down
1. Perkins Institute location
2. Asylum playroom for Annie and Jimmy
3. Negro servant
4. Fetched by James to rescue Annie
5. Torn off Aunt Ev's dress by Helen for doll's eyes
6. Home for Annie and Helen for two weeks: ___ house
7. Thinks half-sister Helen should be in asylum
8. She has not loved a soul since her brother's death
9. Original sin according to Annie: ___ up
10. Driven to pick up Annie at the train station
12. A touch here means Kate
13. A woman steeled in grief
14. Martha and Percy play with paper ___

CROSSWORD ANSWER KEY - Miracle Worker

		1 B	E	L	L		2 D	3 E	4 V	I	L	
		O			5 B	I	T	E		I		A
6 G	I	B	S	O	N		U		A		N		D
A			T			T		D		E		D		7 J
R			O			T		H		Y		E		A
D		8 A	N	9 A	G	N	O	S			10 C	R	A	M	P
E		N		I		N		O			A			E
N		N		V		11 S	12 C	I	S	S	O	R	S	
	13 K	E	Y	I		H		E			R			14 D
	A			N		E					15 I	V	Y		O
	T			G		16 H	E	L	E	N		A			L
17 P	E	R	C	Y		K					G			L
						18 E	Y	E	L	I	D	S

Across
1. Used by Percy to alert family of Helen's outburst
2. Annie called Helen this after she hid the room key
5. Helen does this to her fingers in her mouth
6. Playwright
8. Annie's mentor from Perkins Institute
10. Annie has this from signing to Helen: writer's ___
11. Taken from Martha forcefully by Helen
13. Dropped by Helen into the well
15. Keller estate in Alabama: ___ Green
16. Like a little safe, locked, that no one can open
17. Helen puts her fingers in his mouth
18. Doll blind girls give Annie for Helen has movable ___

Down
1. Perkins Institute location
2. Asylum playroom for Annie and Jimmy
3. Negro servant
4. Fetched by James to rescue Annie
5. Torn off Aunt Ev's dress by Helen for doll's eyes
6. Home for Annie and Helen for two weeks: ___ house
7. Thinks half-sister Helen should be in asylum
8. She has not loved a soul since her brother's death
9. Original sin according to Annie: ___ up
10. Driven to pick up Annie at the train station
12. A touch here means Kate
13. A woman steeled in grief
14. Martha and Percy play with paper ___

MATCHING QUIZ/WORKSHEET 1 - Miracle Worker

___ 1. PERCY A. Used by Percy to alert family of Helen's outburst

___ 2. TOOTH B. Captain wishes Annie would show some

___ 3. FOREVER C. Playwright

___ 4. DOCTOR D. A woman steeled in grief

___ 5. JIMMY E. Governess's age

___ 6. DEADHOUSE F. Sign for Annie

___ 7. GIBSON G. Is to the mind more than light is to the eye

___ 8. KEY H. Anne's last name

___ 9. NEEDLE I. Dropped by Helen into the well

___10. TWENTY J. Driven to pick up Annie at the train station

___11. JAMES K. Fetched by James to rescue Annie

___12. TEACHER L. Breakthrough word for Helen

___13. KELLER M. Thinks half-sister Helen should be in asylum

___14. SULLIVAN N. Asylum playroom for Annie and Jimmy

___15. CARRIAGE O. Haunting voice in Annie's mind

___16. LANGUAGE P. Promise of love to Jimmy and then Helen

___17. RING Q. She has not loved a soul since her brother's death

___18. BELL R. Annie's mentor from Perkins Institute

___19. BITE S. Used to jab Annie

___20. WATER T. Diagnoses baby Helen with acute congestion

___21. ANNE U. Helen does this to her fingers in her mouth

___22. KATE V. Helen puts her fingers in his mouth

___23. ANAGNOS W. It was knocked out when Helen hit Annie with the doll

___24. LADDER X. Views women as the flowers of civilization; Captain ___

___25. PITY Y. Going away present fron Anagnos

KEY: MATCHING QUIZ/WORKSHEET 1 - Miracle Worker

V - 1. PERCY	A.	Used by Percy to alert family of Helen's outburst
W - 2. TOOTH	B.	Captain wishes Annie would show some
P - 3. FOREVER	C.	Playwright
T - 4. DOCTOR	D.	A woman steeled in grief
O - 5. JIMMY	E.	Governess's age
N - 6. DEADHOUSE	F.	Sign for Annie
C - 7. GIBSON	G.	Is to the mind more than light is to the eye
I - 8. KEY	H.	Anne's last name
S - 9. NEEDLE	I.	Dropped by Helen into the well
E - 10. TWENTY	J.	Driven to pick up Annie at the train station
M - 11. JAMES	K.	Fetched by James to rescue Annie
F - 12. TEACHER	L.	Breakthrough word for Helen
X - 13. KELLER	M.	Thinks half-sister Helen should be in asylum
H - 14. SULLIVAN	N.	Asylum playroom for Annie and Jimmy
J - 15. CARRIAGE	O.	Haunting voice in Annie's mind
G - 16. LANGUAGE	P.	Promise of love to Jimmy and then Helen
Y - 17. RING	Q.	She has not loved a soul since her brother's death
A - 18. BELL	R.	Annie's mentor from Perkins Institute
U - 19. BITE	S.	Used to jab Annie
L - 20. WATER	T.	Diagnoses baby Helen with acute congestion
Q - 21. ANNE	U.	Helen does this to her fingers in her mouth
D - 22. KATE	V.	Helen puts her fingers in his mouth
R - 23. ANAGNOS	W.	It was knocked out when Helen hit Annie with the doll
K - 24. LADDER	X.	Views women as the flowers of civilization; Captain ___
B - 25. PITY	Y.	Going away present fron Anagnos

MATCHING QUIZ/WORKSHEET 2 - Miracle Worker

___ 1. BOSTON   A. Doll blind girls give Annie for Helen has movable ___
___ 2. THREE   B. Helen's younger sibling
___ 3. TEWKSBURY   C. Dropped by Helen into the well
___ 4. ANAGNOS   D. Sign for Captain Keller
___ 5. LANGUAGE   E. Is to the mind more than light is to the eye
___ 6. LADDER   F. Annie called Helen this after she hid the room key
___ 7. PERCY   G. Sign for Annie
___ 8. KEY   H. Helen puts her fingers in his mouth
___ 9. KELLER   I. Views women as the flowers of civilization; Captain ___
___10. DOLLS   J. Annie's mentor from Perkins Institute
___11. DEADHOUSE   K. Annie has this from signing to Helen: writer's ___
___12. KATE   L. Haunting voice in Annie's mind
___13. TEACHER   M. Asylum playroom for Annie and Jimmy
___14. EYELIDS   N. Perkins Institute location
___15. PITY   O. Martha and Percy play with paper ___
___16. MOUSETRAP   P. Captain wishes Annie would show some
___17. WATER   Q. Number of acts in this play
___18. GLASSES   R. Breakthrough word for Helen
___19. JIMMY   S. A woman steeled in grief
___20. CRAMP   T. Annie's trademark: smoked ___
___21. TWENTYFIVE   U. A touch here means Kate
___22. CHEEK   V. Institution where Jimmy died
___23. DEVIL   W. Helen's mind worked like one
___24. MILDRED   X. Number of dollars a week Annie is paid
___25. PAPA   Y. Fetched by James to rescue Annie

KEY: MATCHING QUIZ/WORKSHEET 2 - Miracle Worker

N - 1. BOSTON   A. Doll blind girls give Annie for Helen has movable ___
Q - 2. THREE   B. Helen's younger sibling
V - 3. TEWKSBURY   C. Dropped by Helen into the well
J - 4. ANAGNOS   D. Sign for Captain Keller
E - 5. LANGUAGE   E. Is to the mind more than light is to the eye
Y - 6. LADDER   F. Annie called Helen this after she hid the room key
H - 7. PERCY   G. Sign for Annie
C - 8. KEY   H. Helen puts her fingers in his mouth
I - 9. KELLER   I. Views women as the flowers of civilization; Captain ___
O -10. DOLLS   J. Annie's mentor from Perkins Institute
M -11. DEADHOUSE   K. Annie has this from signing to Helen: writer's ___
S -12. KATE   L. Haunting voice in Annie's mind
G -13. TEACHER   M. Asylum playroom for Annie and Jimmy
A -14. EYELIDS   N. Perkins Institute location
P -15. PITY   O. Martha and Percy play with paper ___
W 16. MOUSETRAP   P. Captain wishes Annie would show some
R -17. WATER   Q. Number of acts in this play
T -18. GLASSES   R. Breakthrough word for Helen
L -19. JIMMY   S. A woman steeled in grief
K -20. CRAMP   T. Annie's trademark: smoked ___
X -21. TWENTYFIVE   U. A touch here means Kate
U -22. CHEEK   V. Institution where Jimmy died
F -23. DEVIL   W. Helen's mind worked like one
B -24. MILDRED   X. Number of dollars a week Annie is paid
D -25. PAPA   Y. Fetched by James to rescue Annie

JUGGLE LETTER 1 - Miracle Worker

1. OBSTON = 1. _____
   Perkins Institute location

2. EHTRE = 2. _____
   Number of acts in this play

3. OTOTH = 3. _____
   It was knocked out when Helen hit Annie with the doll

4. NEIEEDCBO = 4. _____
   Gateway through which knowledge enters the mind

5. LEHNE = 5. _____
   Like a little safe, locked, that no one can open

6. NAINPK = 6. _____
   Folded by Helen

7. ESLSGAS = 7. _____
   Annie's trademark: smoked ___

8. NAELG = 8. _____
   Baby Martha

9. SRAT = 9. _____
   Playthings for Annie and Jimmy in asylum

10. RHPITEC =10. _____
    Needed to be refilled at the pump

11. GINVGI =11. _____
    Original sin according to Annie: ___ up

12. PAAP =12. _____
    Sign for Captain Keller

13. VLDEI =13. _____
    Annie called Helen this after she hid the room key

14. EHKCE =14. _____
    A touch here means Kate

15. IEVTWEFNTY =15. _____
    Number of dollars a week Annieis paid

16. LBLE   =16. _____
                   Used by Percy to alert family of Helen's outburst

17. NANE   =17. _____
                   She has not loved a soul since her brother's death

18. EKY   =18. _____
                   Dropped by Helen into the well

19. RDELIDM   =19. _____
                   Helen's younger sibling

20. AIIRTOCDYN   =20. _____
                   Used by Annie to spell correctly

21. TEKA   =21. _____
                   A woman steeled in grief

22. VIY   =22. _____
                   Keller estate in Alabama: ___ Green

23. BSTCAMUUI   =23. _____
                   Town in AL where Kellers reside

24. HAARTM   =24. _____
                   Helen's female Negro playmate

25. YECPR   =25. _____
                   Helen puts her fingers in his mouth

26. MCRPA   =26. _____
                   Annie has this from signing to Helen: writer's ___

27. EOHCCRT   =27. _____
                   Helen made a string of wool doing this craft

28. MEJAS   =28. _____
                   Thinks half-sister Helen should be in asylum

29. EAGIRARC   =29. _____
                   Driven to pick up Annie at the train station

JUGGLE LETTER 1 ANSWER KEY - Miracle Worker

1. OBSTON = 1. BOSTON
Perkins Institute location

2. EHTRE = 2. THREE
Number of acts in this play

3. OTOTH = 3. TOOTH
It was knocked out when Helen hit Annie with the doll

4. NEIEEDCBO = 4. OBEDIENCE
Gateway through which knowledge enters the mind

5. LEHNE = 5. HELEN
Like a little safe, locked, that no one can open

6. NAINPK = 6. NAPKIN
Folded by Helen

7. ESLSGAS = 7. GLASSES
Annie's trademark: smoked ___

8. NAELG = 8. ANGEL
Baby Martha

9. SRAT = 9. RATS
Playthings for Annie and Jimmy in asylum

10. RHPITEC =10. PITCHER
Needed to be refilled at the pump

11. GINVGI =11. GIVING
Original sin according to Annie: ___ up

12. PAAP =12. PAPA
Sign for Captain Keller

13. VLDEI =13. DEVIL
Annie called Helen this after she hid the room key

14. EHKCE =14. CHEEK
A touch here means Kate

15. IEVTWEFNTY =15. TWENTYFIVE
Number of dollars a week Annieis paid

16. LBLE =16. BELL
Used by Percy to alert family of Helen's outburst

17. NANE =17. ANNE
She has not loved a soul since her brother's death

18. EKY =18. KEY
Dropped by Helen into the well

19. RDELIDM =19. MILDRED
Helen's younger sibling

20. AIIRTOCDYN =20. DICTIONARY
Used by Annie to spell correctly

21. TEKA =21. KATE
A woman steeled in grief

22. VIY =22. IVY
Keller estate in Alabama: ___ Green

23. BSTCAMUUI =23. TUSCUMBIA
Town in AL where Kellers reside

24. HAARTM =24. MARTHA
Helen's female Negro playmate

25. YECPR =25. PERCY
Helen puts her fingers in his mouth

26. MCRPA =26. CRAMP
Annie has this from signing to Helen: writer's ___

27. EOHCCRT =27. CROCHET
Helen made a string of wool doing this craft

28. MEJAS =28. JAMES
Thinks half-sister Helen should be in asylum

29. EAGIRARC =29. CARRIAGE
Driven to pick up Annie at the train station

JUGGLE LETTER 2 - Miracle Worker

1. TERWA = 1. _____
   Breakthrough word for Helen

2. KERINSP = 2. _____
   Institute for the blind in Boston

3. ADEEDUOHS = 3. _____
   Asylum playroom for Annie and Jimmy

4. MIMJY = 4. _____
   Haunting voice in Annie's mind

5. IEBT = 5. _____
   Helen does this to her fingers in her mouth

6. IPYT = 6. _____
   Captain wishes Annie would show some

7. ODRCTO = 7. _____
   Diagnoses baby Helen with acute congestion

8. NOANSGA = 8. _____
   Annie's mentor from Perkins Institute

9. UILASVLN = 9. _____
   Anne's last name

10. YWETNT =10. _____
    Governess's age

11. NGERDA =11. _____
    Home for Annie and Helen for two weeks: ___ house

12. EALDRD =12. _____
    Fetched by James to rescue Annie

13. RREVEOF =13. _____
    Promise of love to Jimmy and then Helen

14. DOSLL =14. _____
    Martha and Percy play with paper ___

15. DSEIYEL =15. _____
    Doll blind girls give Annie for Helen has movable ___

16. EDEELN	=16. _____
		Used to jab Annie

17. EHTCREA	=17. _____
		Sign for Annie

18. EATUORSPM	=18. _____
		Helen's mind worked like one

19. LKLEER	=19. _____
		Views women as the flowers of civilization; Captain ___

20. IARTN	=20. _____
		How Annie traveled from Boston to Alabama

21. IYVEN	=21. _____
		Negro servant

22. NIGR	=22. _____
		Going away present fron Anagnos

23. GNLUEAGA	=23. _____
		Is to the mind more than light is to the eye

24. UOTNTSB	=24. _____
		Torn off Aunt Ev's dress by Helen for doll's eyes

25. INGBOS	=25. _____
		Playwright

26. YKBRUEWTS	=26. _____
		Institution where Jimmy died

27. SSIROSCS	=27. _____
		Taken from Martha forcefully by Helen

JUGGLE LETTER 2 ANSWER KEY - Miracle Worker

1. TERWA = 1. WATER
   Breakthrough word for Helen

2. KERINSP = 2. PERKINS
   Institute for the blind in Boston

3. ADEEDUOHS = 3. DEADHOUSE
   Asylum playroom for Annie and Jimmy

4. MIMJY = 4. JIMMY
   Haunting voice in Annie's mind

5. IEBT = 5. BITE
   Helen does this to her fingers in her mouth

6. IPYT = 6. PITY
   Captain wishes Annie would show some

7. ODRCTO = 7. DOCTOR
   Diagnoses baby Helen with acute congestion

8. NOANSGA = 8. ANAGNOS
   Annie's mentor from Perkins Institute

9. UILASVLN = 9. SULLIVAN
   Anne's last name

10. YWETNT =10. TWENTY
    Governess's age

11. NGERDA =11. GARDEN
    Home for Annie and Helen for two weeks: ___ house

12. EALDRD =12. LADDER
    Fetched by James to rescue Annie

13. RREVEOF =13. FOREVER
    Promise of love to Jimmy and then Helen

14. DOSLL =14. DOLLS
    Martha and Percy play with paper ___

15. DSEIYEL =15. EYELIDS
    Doll blind girls give Annie for Helen has movable ___

16. EDEELN =16. NEEDLE
Used to jab Annie

17. EHTCREA =17. TEACHER
Sign for Annie

18. EATUORSPM =18. MOUSETRAP
Helen's mind worked like one

19. LKLEER =19. KELLER
Views women as the flowers of civilization; Captain ___

20. IARTN =20. TRAIN
How Annie traveled from Boston to Alabama

21. IYVEN =21. VINEY
Negro servant

22. NIGR =22. RING
Going away present fron Anagnos

23. GNLUEAGA =23. LANGUAGE
Is to the mind more than light is to the eye

24. UOTNTSB =24. BUTTONS
Torn off Aunt Ev's dress by Helen for doll's eyes

25. INGBOS =25. GIBSON
Playwright

26. YKBRUEWTS =26. TEWKSBURY
Institution where Jimmy died

27. SSIROSCS =27. SCISSORS
Taken from Martha forcefully by Helen

MIRACLE WORKER WORD LIST

No.	Word	Clue/Definition
1.	ANAGNOS	Annie's mentor from Perkins Institute
2.	ANGEL	Baby Martha
3.	ANNE	She has not loved a soul since her brother's death
4.	BELL	Used by Percy to alert family of Helen's outburst
5.	BITE	Helen does this to her fingers in her mouth
6.	BOSTON	Perkins Institute location
7.	BUTTONS	Torn off Aunt Ev's dress by Helen for doll's eyes
8.	CARRIAGE	Driven to pick up Annie at the train station
9.	CHEEK	A touch here means Kate
10.	CRAMP	Annie has this from signing to Helen: writer's ___
11.	CROCHET	Helen made a string of wool doing this craft
12.	DEADHOUSE	Asylum playroom for Annie and Jimmy
13.	DEVIL	Annie called Helen this after she hid the room key
14.	DICTIONARY	Used by Annie to spell correctly
15.	DOCTOR	Diagnoses baby Helen with acute congestion
16.	DOLLS	Martha and Percy play with paper ___
17.	EYELIDS	Doll blind girls give Annie for Helen has movable ___
18.	FOREVER	Promise of love to Jimmy and then Helen
19.	GARDEN	Home for Annie and Helen for two weeks: ___ house
20.	GIBSON	Playwright
21.	GIVING	Original sin according to Annie: ___ up
22.	GLASSES	Annie's trademark: smoked ___
23.	HELEN	Like a little safe, locked, that no one can open
24.	IVY	Keller estate in Alabama: ___ Green
25.	JAMES	Thinks half-sister Helen should be in asylum
26.	JIMMY	Haunting voice in Annie's mind
27.	KATE	A woman steeled in grief
28.	KELLER	Views women as the flowers of civilization; Captain ___
29.	KEY	Dropped by Helen into the well
30.	LADDER	Fetched by James to rescue Annie
31.	LANGUAGE	Is to the mind more than light is to the eye
32.	MARTHA	Helen's female Negro playmate
33.	MILDRED	Helen's younger sibling
34.	MOUSETRAP	Helen's mind worked like one
35.	NAPKIN	Folded by Helen
36.	NEEDLE	Used to jab Annie
37.	OBEDIENCE	Gateway through which knowledge enters the mind
38.	PAPA	Sign for Captain Keller
39.	PERCY	Helen puts her fingers in his mouth
40.	PERKINS	Institute for the blind in Boston
41.	PITCHER	Needed to be refilled at the pump
42.	PITY	Captain wishes Annie would show some
43.	RATS	Playthings for Annie and Jimmy in asylum
44.	RING	Going away present fron Anagnos
45.	SCISSORS	Taken from Martha forcefully by Helen
46.	SULLIVAN	Anne's last name
47.	TEACHER	Sign for Annie
48.	TEWKSBURY	Institution where Jimmy died
49.	THREE	Number of acts in this play
50.	TOOTH	It was knocked out when Helen hit Annie with the doll

MIRACLE WORKER WORD LIST continued

No.	Word	Clue/Definition
51.	TRAIN	How Annie traveled from Boston to Alabama
52.	TUSCUMBIA	Town in AL where Kellers reside
53.	TWENTY	Governess's age
54.	TWENTYFIVE	Number of dollars a week Annieis paid
55.	VINEY	Negro servant
56.	WATER	Breakthrough word for Helen

VOCABULARY RESOURCE MATERIALS

VOCABULARY WORD SEARCH - Miracle Worker

```
I M P A S S I V E L Y P R O F F E R E D
N N L T N T D E M A L U R M F L I E G R
T M A Y O N E X P M B M O I M I M T A Q
E T I R I E S E H E A M B N M N P S G B
R R N A T N I D A N R E S O I E E N N H
P A T N A I C L T T O L T U N F R I E R
O C I T M T C Y I S X S I S D F C P S Q
S H V G I R A U C Z E P N L U E E S I N
E O E R T E T N L L N D A Y L C P M D D
S M L X N P E K N A I X T Z G T T O M C
C A Y I I M D E E I T N E Y E U I R V M
N O F F C I X M T V Q E D C N A B O A Y
R W M G O I J P T O J I V O T L L S L C
I T L P C R T T L J W B M K L J Y E I O
M E H S U P L U E X I M D P H E T L A M
P M T U L N Q O D Z T Z A T U A N Y N B
E P H O I M C Z R E H V D Q M D L T T A
R E A I S B W T L N E S O M X D E Z L T
I R G C T E P I I R R X U G N J L N Y I
O A G A Y N G Q S O I S R A Z C C F C V
U N A V A I L I N G N A L M S H O U S E
S C R I V G O F W O G B Y W R I T H E S
J E D V B N Q D C P L A C A T I N G R G
```

ALMSHOUSE	IMPASSIVELY	LAMENTS	TEMPERANCE
AVERSION	IMPERCEPTIBLY	MOROSELY	TRACHOMA
BENIGN	IMPERIOUS	NETTLED	TYRANT
BLANDLY	IMPERTINENT	OBSTINATE	UNAVAILING
COMBATIVE	IMPUDENCE	OCULIST	UNKEMPT
COMPUNCTION	INARTICULATE	OMINOUSLY	VALIANTLY
CONSUMMATELY	INDOLENT	PLACATING	VEXEDLY
DESICCATED	INDULGENT	PLAINTIVELY	VIGIL
DISENGAGE	INEFFECTUAL	PRIMER	VIVACIOUS
DOURLY	INEXORABLY	PROFFERED	WITHERING
EMPHATIC	INTERPOSES	PUMMELS	WRITHES
FORLORN	INTIMATIONS	SOLICITUDE	
HAGGARD	JOVIAL	SPINSTER	

VOCABULARY WORD SEARCH ANSWER KEY - Miracle Worker

ALMSHOUSE	IMPASSIVELY	LAMENTS	TEMPERANCE
AVERSION	IMPERCEPTIBLY	MOROSELY	TRACHOMA
BENIGN	IMPERIOUS	NETTLED	TYRANT
BLANDLY	IMPERTINENT	OBSTINATE	UNAVAILING
COMBATIVE	IMPUDENCE	OCULIST	UNKEMPT
COMPUNCTION	INARTICULATE	OMINOUSLY	VALIANTLY
CONSUMMATELY	INDOLENT	PLACATING	VEXEDLY
DESICCATED	INDULGENT	PLAINTIVELY	VIGIL
DISENGAGE	INEFFECTUAL	PRIMER	VIVACIOUS
DOURLY	INEXORABLY	PROFFERED	WITHERING
EMPHATIC	INTERPOSES	PUMMELS	WRITHES
FORLORN	INTIMATIONS	SOLICITUDE	
HAGGARD	JOVIAL	SPINSTER	

VOCABULARY CROSSWORD - Miracle Worker

Across
1. Somewhat ill-tempered
4. A watch
7. Unnoticeably; barely
10. Disorderly; messy
11. Sanitarium
13. Flatly; tritely
14. Hardship; problem
15. Moans; wails
16. Satisfying; gratifying

Down
1. Evaluation
2. Manual; handbook
3. Harsh, cruel leader
5. Unending; ceaseless
6. Favorable; harmless
8. Confused; bewildered
9. Obliged; made responsible
11. Agreeably; willingly
12. Drearily

VOCABULARY CROSSWORD ANSWER KEY - Miracle Worker

	1 A	2 S	P	E	R	3 I	T	Y		4 V	5 I	G	I	L
	P		R			Y			6 B		N			
	P		7 I	M	P	E	R	C	E	P	T	8 I	B	L	Y
	R		M			A			N		E		A		
	A		E			N			I		R		F		9 C
	I		R			T			G		M		F		O
	S								N		I		L		M
	A									10 U	N	K	E	M	P	T
11 A	L	M	S	H	O	U	S	E			A		D		E
M											B				L
I								12 D		13 B	L	A	N	D	L	Y
14 A	F	F	L	I	C	T	I	O	N		E				E
B								U							D
15 L	A	M	E	N	T	S		R							
Y							16 P	L	A	C	A	T	I	N	G
							Y							

Across
1. Somewhat ill-tempered
4. A watch
7. Unnoticeably; barely
10. Disorderly; messy
11. Sanitarium
13. Flatly; tritely
14. Hardship; problem
15. Moans; wails
16. Satisfying; gratifying

Down
1. Evaluation
2. Manual; handbook
3. Harsh, cruel leader
5. Unending; ceaseless
6. Favorable; harmless
8. Confused; bewildered
9. Obliged; made responsible
11. Agreeably; willingly
12. Drearily

VOCABULARY WORKSHEET 1 - *The Miracle Worker*

____ 1. DESICCATED   A. Resigns; gives up

____ 2. UNAVAILING   B. Wrapped up

____ 3. WITHERING   C. Clearly; obviously

____ 4. INEXORABLY   D. Shrinking; shriveling

____ 5. SWADDLED   E. Confused; bewildered

____ 6. WRITHES   F. Dried up

____ 7. FRIVOLOUS   G. Unnoticeably; barely

____ 8. INTIMATIONS   H. Twists from pain; flails

____ 9. CONSPICUOUSLY   I. Sanitarium

____ 10. WOEBEGONE   J. Drearily

____ 11. APPRAISAL   K. Thrashes; beats

____ 12. UNKEMPT   L. Trivial; petty

____ 13. IMPUDENCE   M. Hopeless; futile

____ 14. RELINQUISHES   N. Relentlessly; unyielding

____ 15. IMPERCEPTIBLY   O. Miserable; sorrowful

____ 16. ALMSHOUSE   P. Disorderly; messy

____ 17. DOURLY   Q. Inflammation of the eyelids

____ 18. BAFFLED   R. Allusions; hints

____ 19. PUMMELS   S. Boldness

____ 20. TRACHOMA   T. Evaluation

KEY: VOCABULARY WORKSHEET 1 - *The Miracle Worker*

F - 1. DESICCATED		A. Resigns; gives up
M - 2. UNAVAILING		B. Wrapped up
D - 3. WITHERING		C. Clearly; obviously
N - 4. INEXORABLY		D. Shrinking; shriveling
B - 5. SWADDLED		E. Confused; bewildered
H - 6. WRITHES		F. Dried up
L - 7. FRIVOLOUS		G. Unnoticeably; barely
R - 8. INTIMATIONS		H. Twists from pain; flails
C - 9. CONSPICUOUSLY		I. Sanitarium
O - 10. WOEBEGONE		J. Drearily
T - 11. APPRAISAL		K. Thrashes; beats
P - 12. UNKEMPT		L. Trivial; petty
S - 13. IMPUDENCE		M. Hopeless; futile
A - 14. RELINQUISHES		N. Relentlessly; unyielding
G - 15. IMPERCEPTIBLY		O. Miserable; sorrowful
I - 16. ALMSHOUSE		P. Disorderly; messy
J - 17. DOURLY		Q. Inflammation of the eyelids
E - 18. BAFFLED		R. Allusions; hints
K - 19. PUMMELS		S. Boldness
Q - 20. TRACHOMA		T. Evaluation

VOCABULARY WORKSHEET 2 - *The Miracle Worker*

____ 1. REPROACHFULLY   A. Sorrowfully; sadly

____ 2. DEPRIVATION   B. Motionless; frozen

____ 3. AFFLICTION   C. Allusions; hints

____ 4. CONSUMMATELY   D. Bothered; peeved

____ 5. INDIGNANTLY   E. Righteously angry

____ 6. PUMMELS   F. Unending; ceaseless

____ 7. IMPERIOUS   G. Satisfying; gratifying

____ 8. TRANSFIXED   H. Disapprovingly; critically

____ 9. OCULIST   I. Drearily

____ 10. INTIMATIONS   J. Evaluation

____ 11. DEFERENTIAL   K. Respectful; obedient

____ 12. NETTLED   L. Absolutely; perfectly

____ 13. INTERMINABLE   M. Eye doctor

____ 14. AVERSION   N. Lively; spirited

____ 15. DEVOUTNESS   O. Loss

____ 16. PLAINTIVELY   P. Thrashes; beats

____ 17. PLACATING   Q. Distaste; dislike

____ 18. VIVACIOUS   R. Hardship; problem

____ 19. DOURLY   S. Godliness; piety

____ 20. APPRAISAL   T. Urgent; pressing

KEY: VOCABULARY WORKSHEET 2 - *The Miracle Worker*

H - 1. REPROACHFULLY	A. Sorrowfully; sadly
O - 2. DEPRIVATION	B. Motionless; frozen
R - 3. AFFLICTION	C. Allusions; hints
L - 4. CONSUMMATELY	D. Bothered; peeved
E - 5. INDIGNANTLY	E. Righteously angry
P - 6. PUMMELS	F. Unending; ceaseless
T - 7. IMPERIOUS	G. Satisfying; gratifying
B - 8. TRANSFIXED	H. Disapprovingly; critically
M - 9. OCULIST	I. Drearily
C - 10. INTIMATIONS	J. Evaluation
K - 11. DEFERENTIAL	K. Respectful; obedient
D - 12. NETTLED	L. Absolutely; perfectly
F - 13. INTERMINABLE	M. Eye doctor
Q - 14. AVERSION	N. Lively; spirited
S - 15. DEVOUTNESS	O. Loss
A - 16. PLAINTIVELY	P. Thrashes; beats
G - 17. PLACATING	Q. Distaste; dislike
N - 18. VIVACIOUS	R. Hardship; problem
I - 19. DOURLY	S. Godliness, piety
J - 20. APPRAISAL	T. Urgent; pressing

VOCABULARY JUGGLE LETTER 1 - Miracle Worker

1. MEECCREODMN = 1. _____
   Repeated; began again

2. LEPCODLEM = 2. _____
   Obliged; made responsible

3. NACIOTFLIF = 3. _____
   Hardship; problem

4. RMTHAOCA = 4. _____
   Inflammation of the eyelids

5. YLNTVAILA = 5. _____
   Bravely; courageously

6. IABMLAY = 6. _____
   Agreeably; willingly

7. PCUOCSNUSIYLO = 7. _____
   Clearly; obviously

8. IRENTSPS = 8. _____
   Old, unmarried woman

9. GOENOWBEE = 9. _____
   Miserable; sorrowful

10. EATRICRCUA = 10. _____
    Exaggerated model

11. RPMEIR = 11. _____
    Manual; handbook

12. LTBAMIENINER = 12. _____
    Unending; ceaseless

13. CITLSOU = 13. _____
    Eye doctor

14. APRALASIP = 14. _____
    Evaluation

15. TDRUNPEUBRE = 15. _____
    Undisturbed; unbothered

16. ESNTUSOEVD =16. _____
Godliness; piety

17. EFBDAFL =17. _____
Confused; bewildered

18. INXTSFEARD =18. _____
Motionless; frozen

19. GINEBN =19. _____
Favorable; harmless

20. USOLELYRTE =20. _____
Deliberately; willfully

21. MCAIHTEP =21. _____
Pointed; insistent

22. NELMAST =22. _____
Moans; wails

23. LSEPYIIMVAS =23. _____
Unemotionally

24. ATUILNFECEF =24. _____
Useless

25. EAOHMULSS =25. _____
Sanitarium

26. VMECOIBTA =26. _____
Inclined to fight

27. NDIEUCEMP =27. _____
Boldness

28. NNIAVIGAUL =28. _____
Hopeless; futile

29. NAITCYBLTAR =29. _____
Inflexibly; in a headstrong manner

30. ITPELLINAVY =30. _____
Sorrowfully; sadly

31. AOVLIJ =31. _____
Jolly; happy

32. TUILDEGNN =32. _____
Permissive; lenient

33. HERSEIISNLQU =33. _____
Resigns; gives up

34. AYIFOECTSLU =34. _____
Flippant; smart-alecky

35. AEDLWSDD =35. _____
Wrapped up

36. MTMNAIEOP =36. _____
Gestures without voice

37. FFEORDPRE =37. _____
Offered forth

38. OUOLYINMS =38. _____
Threateningly; darkly; gloomily

39. MYAXSROP =39. _____
Fit; attack

40. CIOTILUEDS =40. _____
Concern

41. NULTIAIARTCE =41. _____
Wordless; silent

42. MSCNOAEUMTLY =42. _____
Absolutely; perfectly

43. ESCITDCADE =43. _____
Dried up

VOCABULARY JUGGLE LETTER 1 ANSWER KEY - Miracle Worker

1. MEECCREODMN = 1. RECOMMENCED
   Repeated; began again

2. LEPCODLEM = 2. COMPELLED
   Obliged; made responsible

3. NACIOTFLIF = 3. AFFLICTION
   Hardship; problem

4. RMTHAOCA = 4. TRACHOMA
   Inflammation of the eyelids

5. YLNTVAILA = 5. VALIANTLY
   Bravely; courageously

6. IABMLAY = 6. AMIABLY
   Agreeably; willingly

7. PCUOCSNUSIYLO = 7. CONSPICUOUSLY
   Clearly; obviously

8. IRENTSPS = 8. SPINSTER
   Old, unmarried woman

9. GOENOWBEE = 9. WOEBEGONE
   Miserable; sorrowful

10. EATRICRCUA = 10. CARICATURE
    Exaggerated model

11. RPMEIR = 11. PRIMER
    Manual; handbook

12. LTBAMIENINER = 12. INTERMINABLE
    Unending; ceaseless

13. CITLSOU = 13. OCULIST
    Eye doctor

14. APRALASIP = 14. APPRAISAL
    Evaluation

15. TDRUNPEUBRE = 15. UNPERTURBED
    Undisturbed; unbothered

16. ESNTUSOEVD	=16.	**DEVOUTNESS**
		Godliness; piety
17. EFBDAFL	=17.	**BAFFLED**
		Confused; bewildered
18. INXTSFEARD	=18.	**TRANSFIXED**
		Motionless; frozen
19. GINEBN	=19.	**BENIGN**
		Favorable; harmless
20. USOLELYRTE	=20.	**RESOLUTELY**
		Deliberately; willfully
21. MCAIHTEP	=21.	**EMPHATIC**
		Pointed; insistent
22. NELMAST	=22.	**LAMENTS**
		Moans; wails
23. LSEPYIIMVAS	=23.	**IMPASSIVELY**
		Unemotionally
24. ATUILNFECEF	=24.	**INEFFECTUAL**
		Useless
25. EAOHMULSS	=25.	**ALMSHOUSE**
		Sanitarium
26. VMECOIBTA	=26.	**COMBATIVE**
		Inclined to fight
27. NDIEUCEMP	=27.	**IMPUDENCE**
		Boldness
28. NNIAVIGAUL	=28.	**UNAVAILING**
		Hopeless; futile
29. NAITCYBLTAR	=29.	**INTRACTABLY**
		Inflexibly; in a headstrong manner
30. ITPELLINAVY	=30.	**PLAINTIVELY**
		Sorrowfully; sadly
31. AOVLIJ	=31.	**JOVIAL**
		Jolly; happy
32. TUILDEGNN	=32.	**INDULGENT**
		Permissive; lenient

33. HERSEIISNLQU =33. RELINQUISHES
Resigns; gives up

34. AYIFOECTSLU =34. FACETIOUSLY
Flippant; smart-alecky

35. AEDLWSDD =35. SWADDLED
Wrapped up

36. MTMNAIEOP =36. PANTOMIME
Gestures without voice

37. FFEORDPRE =37. PROFFERED
Offered forth

38. OUOLYINMS =38. OMINOUSLY
Threateningly; darkly; gloomily

39. MYAXSROP =39. PAROXYSM
Fit; attack

40. CIOTILUEDS =40. SOLICITUDE
Concern

41. NULTIAIARTCE =41. INARTICULATE
Wordless; silent

42. MSCNOAEUMTLY =42. CONSUMMATELY
Absolutely; perfectly

43. ESCITDCADE =43. DESICCATED
Dried up

VOCABULARY JUGGLE LETTER 2 - Miracle Worker

1. PERNEAEMCT = 1. _____
   Moderation

2. TLEETND = 2. _____
   Bothered; peeved

3. NLEATDIERFE = 3. _____
   Respectful; obedient

4. TLPNICAAG = 4. _____
   Satisfying; gratifying

5. SHUVCAOILR = 5. _____
   Gentlemanly; gallant

6. IVLIG = 6. _____
   A watch

7. SVIDHDEELE = 7. _____
   Rumpled; untidy

8. HREISTW = 8. _____
   Twists from pain; flails

9. OFILUORSV = 9. _____
   Trivial; petty

10. UOVIUNSMOL = 10. _____
    Bulky; large

11. ETINTPNMIER = 11. _____
    Rude; impolite

12. YGIANDLTINN = 12. _____
    Righteously angry

13. IDINUEVTIM = 13. _____
    Small

14. TPRSSEIENO = 14. _____
    Intervenes; interferes

15. ENTUPKM = 15. _____
    Disorderly; messy

16. VPOEITDIRAN =16. _____
Loss

17. ANTTOEIPRID =17. _____
Fear; alarm

18. EXVDELY =18. _____
Irritatedly

19. ITMNUAPALSE =19. _____
Maneuvers; moves

20. RALIXYOEBN =20. _____
Relentlessly; unyielding

21. NIEGEASDG =21. _____
Release; undo

22. CVSIOAUIV =22. _____
Lively; spirited

23. ATMININOSTI =23. _____
Allusions; hints

24. MERYOLSO =24. _____
Gloomily; sullenly

25. BYADLLN =25. _____
Flatly; tritely

26. RLOOFNR =26. _____
Forsaken; abandoned

27. SOVERNAI =27. _____
Distaste for; dislike for

28. YTTNAR =28. _____
Harsh, cruel leader

29. OCPYRHLEFARUL =29. _____
Disapprovingly; critically

30. RLPPYBMTEICIE =30. _____
Unnoticeably; barely

31. UTEESORRLI =31. _____
Uncertain; hesitant

32. BTSOITENA =32. _____
Stubborn; headstrong

33. SIEURMIOP =33. _____
Urgent; pressing

34. ASETPIYR =34. _____
Somewhat ill-tempered

35. ENUSPDONL =35. _____
Bewildered; puzzled

36. ONNCCPMTIOU =36. _____
Shame; regret

37. DLRUOY =37. _____
Drearily

38. IIWTGNERH =38. _____
Shrinking

39. GHGDARA =39. _____
Care worn; drawn

40. LMSPUEM =40. _____
Thrashes; beats

41. UBTRDSCUOETN =41. _____
In open view

42. LNOITNED =42. _____
Idle; inactive

VOCABULARY JUGGLE LETTER 2 - Miracle Worker

1. PERNEAEMCT = 1. TEMPERANCE
   Moderation

2. TLEETND = 2. NETTLED
   Bothered; peeved

3. NLEATDIERFE = 3. DEFERENTIAL
   Respectful; obedient

4. TLPNICAAG = 4. PLACATING
   Satisfying; gratifying

5. SHUVCAOILR = 5. CHIVALROUS
   Gentlemanly; gallant

6. IVLIG = 6. VIGIL
   A watch

7. SVIDHDEELE = 7. DISHEVELED
   Rumpled; untidy

8. HREISTW = 8. WRITHES
   Twists from pain; flails

9. OFILUORSV = 9. FRIVOLOUS
   Trivial; petty

10. UOVIUNSMOL =10. VOLUMINOUS
    Bulky; large

11. ETINTPNMIER =11. IMPERTINENT
    Rude; impolite

12. YGIANDLTINN =12. INDIGNANTLY
    Righteously angry

13. IDINUEVTIM =13. DIMINUTIVE
    Small

14. TPRSSEIENO =14. INTERPOSES
    Intervenes; interferes

15. ENTUPKM =15. UNKEMPT
    Disorderly; messy

16. VPOEITDIRAN =16. DEPRIVATION
Loss

17. ANTTOEIPRID =17. TREPIDATION
Fear; alarm

18. EXVDELY =18. VEXEDLY
Irritatedly

19. ITMNUAPALSE =19. MANIPULATES
Maneuvers; moves

20. RALIXYOEBN =20. INEXORABLY
Relentlessly; unyielding

21. NIEGEASDG =21. DISENGAGE
Release; undo

22. CVSIOAUIV =22. VIVACIOUS
Lively; spirited

23. ATMININOSTI =23. INTIMATIONS
Allusions; hints

24. MERYOLSO =24. MOROSELY
Gloomily; sullenly

25. BYADLLN =25. BLANDLY
Flatly; tritely

26. RLOOFNR =26. FORLORN
Forsaken; abandoned

27. SOVERNAI =27. AVERSION
Distaste for; dislike for

28. YTTNAR =28. TYRANT
Harsh, cruel leader

29. OCPYRHLEFARUL =29. REPROACHFULLY
Disapprovingly; critically

30. RLPPYBMTEICIE =30. IMPERCEPTIBLY
Unnoticeably; barely

31. UTEESORRLI =31. IRRESOLUTE
Uncertain; hesitant

32. BTSOITENA =32. OBSTINATE
Stubborn; headstrong

33. SIEURMIOP =33. IMPERIOUS
Urgent; pressing

34. ASETPIYR =34. ASPERITY
Somewhat ill-tempered

35. ENUSPDONL =35. NONPLUSED
Bewildered; puzzled

36. ONNCCPMTIOU =36. COMPUNCTION
Shame; regret

37. DLRUOY =37. DOURLY
Drearily

38. IIWTGNERH =38. WITHERING
Shrinking

39. GHGDARA =39. HAGGARD
Care worn; drawn

40. LMSPUEM =40. PUMMELS
Thrashes; beats

41. UBTRDSCUOETN =41. UNOBSTRUCTED
In open view

42. LNOITNED =42. INDOLENT
Idle; inactive

MIRACLE WORKER VOCABULARY WORD LIST

No. Word	Clue/Definition
1. AFFLICTION	Hardship; problem
2. ALMSHOUSE	Sanitarium
3. AMIABLY	Agreeably; willingly
4. APPRAISAL	Evaluation
5. ASPERITY	Somewhat ill-tempered
6. AVERSION	Distaste for; dislike for
7. BAFFLED	Confused; bewildered
8. BENIGN	Favorable; harmless
9. BLANDLY	Flatly; tritely
10. CARICATURE	Exaggerated model
11. CHIVALROUS	Gentlemanly; gallant
12. COMBATIVE	Inclined to fight
13. COMPELLED	Obliged; made responsible
14. COMPUNCTION	Shame; regret
15. CONSPICUOUSLY	Clearly; obviously
16. CONSUMMATELY	Absolutely; perfectly
17. DEFERENTIAL	Respectful; obedient
18. DEPRIVATION	Loss
19. DESICCATED	Dried up
20. DEVOUTNESS	Godliness; piety
21. DIMINUTIVE	Small
22. DISENGAGE	Release; undo
23. DISHEVELED	Rumpled; untidy
24. DOURLY	Drearily
25. EMPHATIC	Pointed; insistent
26. FACETIOUSLY	Flippant; smart-alecky
27. FORLORN	Forsaken; abandoned
28. FRIVOLOUS	Trivial; petty
29. HAGGARD	Care worn; drawn
30. IMPASSIVELY	Unemotionally
31. IMPERCEPTIBLY	Unnoticeably; barely
32. IMPERIOUS	Urgent; pressing
33. IMPERTINENT	Rude; impolite
34. IMPUDENCE	Boldness
35. INARTICULATE	Wordless; silent
36. INDIGNANTLY	Righteously angry
37. INDOLENT	Idle; inactive
38. INDULGENT	Permissive; lenient
39. INEFFECTUAL	Useless
40. INEXORABLY	Relentlessly; unyielding
41. INTERMINABLE	Unending; ceaseless
42. INTERPOSES	Intervenes; interferes
43. INTIMATIONS	Allusions; hints
44. INTRACTABLY	Inflexibly; in a headstrong manner
45. IRRESOLUTE	Uncertain; hesitant
46. JOVIAL	Jolly; happy
47. LAMENTS	Moans; wails
48. MANIPULATES	Maneuvers; moves
49. MOROSELY	Gloomily; sullenly

MIRACLE WORKER VOCABULARY WORD LIST continued

No. Word	Clue/Definition
50. NETTLED	Bothered; peeved
51. NONPLUSED	Bewildered; puzzled
52. OBSTINATE	Stubborn; headstrong
53. OCULIST	Eye doctor
54. OMINOUSLY	Threateningly; darkly; gloomily
55. PANTOMIME	Gestures without voice
56. PAROXYSM	Fit; attack
57. PLACATING	Satisfying; gratifying
58. PLAINTIVELY	Sorrowfully; sadly
59. PRIMER	Manual; handbook
60. PROFFERED	Offered forth
61. PUMMELS	Thrashes; beats
62. RECOMMENCED	Repeated; began again
63. RELINQUISHES	Resigns; gives up
64. REPROACHFULLY	Disapprovingly; critically
65. RESOLUTELY	Deliberately; willfully
66. SOLICITUDE	Concern
67. SPINSTER	Old, unmarried woman
68. SWADDLED	Wrapped up
69. TEMPERANCE	Moderation
70. TRACHOMA	Inflammation of the eyelids
71. TRANSFIXED	Motionless; frozen
72. TREPIDATION	Fear; alarm
73. TYRANT	Harsh, cruel leader
74. UNAVAILING	Hopeless; futile
75. UNKEMPT	Disorderly; messy
76. UNOBSTRUCTED	In open view
77. UNPERTURBED	Undisturbed; unbothered
78. VALIANTLY	Bravely; courageously
79. VEXEDLY	Irritatedly
80. VIGIL	A watch
81. VIVACIOUS	Lively; spirited
82. VOLUMINOUS	Bulky; large
83. WITHERING	Shrinking
84. WOEBEGONE	Miserable; sorrowful
85. WRITHES	Twists from pain; flails